The People's History

Sunderland's
Blitz

by

Kevin Brady

Firemen at work, close to the corner of Athenaeum Street and Fawcett Street, April 1941.

Previous page: A resident of the Cleveland Road area salvaging belongings from his wrecked home after the raid of 14th March 1943. Note the Union Jack flag in centre of picture amongst the debris.

Copyright © Kevin Brady 1999

First published in 1999 by

The People's History Ltd
Suite 1
Byron House
Seaham Grange Business Park
Seaham
Co. Durham
SR7 0PY

ISBN 1 902527 55 0

Contents

German reconassiance photograph from August 1939. Taken just 21 days before the outbreak of war.

Introduction

Shortly before midnight on Saturday, 1st April 1916, a new form of warfare arrived in Sunderland – the air raid. Bombing from the air placed the civilian in the front line. Previously it was the soldier and sailor who fought the battles and endured the hardships of war. Now the workers and their families had become the target.

On that April Saturday, many people witnessed 'a cigar shaped object' or a Zeppelin airship ('like a great silver bird') over Sunderland. A number of bombs were dropped on the town, killing 22 people. Twenty-five people were seriously injured and 103 slightly injured. This was an introduction of what was to come in the next conflict.

This project started as an attempt to put names, dates and locations to a number of photographs and glass plate negatives in the *Sunderland Echo* photographic department and library.

Having access to the police files on the air raids I have attempted to match these accounts with documents held at Tyne & Wear Archives at Blandford House, Newcastle and with stories published in the *Echo* with the photographs.

I have also contacted several individuals who have kindly given advice or pointed me in the direction of a further source of information. These individuals include local and national historians, retired and serving officers of the Royal Air Force up to the rank of Air Vice Marshall.

The casualties mentioned in the book are taken from four sources: from lists made immediately after a raid, death notices in the *Echo* from the days after a raid, an official council list, in book form which has some omissions held at Sunderland Central Library, and another list, again held at the Library, which is part of a national register. None of these lists tally. Some have less names, others more. Every effort has been made to find every fatality in Sunderland's air raids, but some people may have been included, but had survived and others may have been missed.

44 & 45 Francis Street, Roker, 14th March 1941.

Acknowledgements

Thanks go to Carol Roberton, Peter Gibson, Maurice Boyle, Neil Mearns, Peter Hepplewhite, Rob Ford, North East Press, Phil Hall & Staff of Sunderland Central Library (Local Studies), Tyne & Wear Archives, Durham Police, Durham County Archives, Durham City Library, Imperial War Museum, Royal Air Force Museum, Air Historical Branch, Ministry of Defence. Richard Watson, Mrs O. Stoddart, Monkwearmouth Local History Group, John Perrin ex-Royal Observer Corps, the late Gordon Holmes, Geoff Snowball, and not forgetting my wife Debbie, daughter Nicola and my mum Marion for their patience and encouragment.

Special thanks to the following for allowing use of their photographs in this publication:

Sunderland Echo
City of Sunderland Libraries
John Yearnshire

Dedicated to my late father Maurice Brady.

The ruins of Victoria Hall after the raid of 15/16th April 1941.

QUIET BEFORE
THE STORM
1939

Searchlight battery, at Dykelands Road TA Centre, 1938. The dishes in the foreground are sound locaters, the searchlight can be seen in the background.

'I am speaking to you from the Cabinet Room of 10 Downing Street. This morning the British Ambassador in Berlin handed the German Government a final note stating that unless we had heard from them by eleven o'clock that they were prepared to withdraw their troops from Poland, a state of war would exist between us. I have to tell you now that no such undertaking has been received, and that consequently this nation is at war with Germany.'

Chamberlain had hardly finished his radio broadcast when the air raid sirens sounded, all across the country. However, the expected aerial onslaught did not materialise, and didn't, in Sunderland at least, for another 10 months. This unexpected non-arrival of the German Air Force, or Luftwaffe, was most welcome, not only to the armed forces, but also for the civilian Air Raid Precautions service.

Preparations

The seeds of the ARP were sown during the First World War, when German aircraft and Zeppelin airships bombed targets in Britain. While London was the main target for these attacks with almost 1,500 people being killed, other cities and towns suffered from this new form of warfare, including Sunderland on Saturday, 1st April 1916.

Some believed that air raids would not only cause material damage, but could also weaken the morale of the civilian population, which, under constant bombardment, could be shattered, consequently bringing defeat.

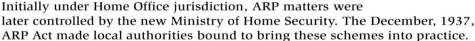

By 1937, with the Spanish Civil War and the knowledge that Germany's rearmament was well underway, so called 'experts' ably assisted by scientists, journalists and those who had witnessed fighting in Spain at first hand, envisaged that London alone could suffer some 200,000 casualties in the first week of hostilities, or 20,000 killed for every raid by 500 bomber aircraft.

Statistics such as these had one positive result in that it prompted the population into some kind of preparation.

In 1935 the ARP (renamed Civil Defence in September 1941) was officially brought into existence when the Government established a Home Office ARP department, with the aim of planning methods to deal with the effects of bombing and possibly gas attacks, as well as the protection from and the aftermath of such attacks.

Air Raid Warden's badge, September 1938.

Initially under Home Office jurisdiction, ARP matters were later controlled by the new Ministry of Home Security. The December, 1937, ARP Act made local authorities bound to bring these schemes into practice.

The country was divided into twelve regions, with No 1 Region being the Northern, its boundaries stretching from the Scottish Border to a point just north of York and to the western boundaries of Northumberland and Durham. The headquarters were situated in Newcastle.

Sunderland ARP, using the stipulated Home Office guidelines, established their control centre at Thornholme, a large house situated on the corner of Thornhill Road and Tunstall Road, currently being used by Thornhill Park School Autistic Unit.

During an alert, two reserve control centres, one at Redby School in Fulwell and the other at No 1 The Esplanade, were kept fully manned keeping in contact with Thornholme every 5 minutes and if there was no reply they had to assume that they were out of action. A messenger would then be dispatched to ascertain if Thornholme was still functioning. Any Thornholme staff member who survived an attack was expected to report immediately to a reserve centre.

Town Clerk and ARP Controller Mr McIntire.

The ARP controller for Sunderland throughout the war was town clerk George McIntire. His reserve was Borough Engineer J.E Lewis. An emergency committee was established which comprised the Mayor, his deputy, an alderman and three councillors.

Contact had to be kept, not only within the borough, but also with the regional ARP controller in Newcastle and neighbouring areas. To this end, five emergency switchboards were set up at the Sunderland telephone exchange, one at The Cedars, off Ryhope Road, and one at East Boldon. Many local firms, in the co-operative spirit of the day, organised their own switchboard to enable them to be used by each other and in an emergency by the local authority.

In the event of Sunderland's ARP being swamped during a heavy raid, a regional co-operation scheme existed whereby neighbouring services could be requested, and were, many times during raids on Sunderland, with a reciprocal

Telephonists at ARP headquarters at Thornholme.

Police saw to the training of wardens, here making adjustments to the military type gas mask, November 1937.

arrangement for Sunderland services. If summoned, outside ARP teams had three rendezvous points to travel to: at Newcastle Road highways depot, at Barley Mow rescue and demolition depot and at Plains Farm depot. Each of these depots had a person in charge, seeing to the opening of facilities on each alert being sounded and ensuring ample parking space, telephone, air raid shelter, food and refreshments were available for the visiting crews. Similar rendezvous points were located throughout the Northern Region and nationwide.

Mainstay of the ARP was the Air Raid Warden. Trained and controlled by the police, the warden was usually allocated a sector, normally a street or ideally a set number of houses and if possible where he or she lived. They had to be completely familiar with their own sector, knowing how many persons occupied any one house and where they could be located in the event of a raid. This could be in a garden shelter, or table shelter and if so situated in which room, or a public

A warden making his report from a telephone box, September 1939.

shelter, so time would not be wasted digging amongst ruins for someone who had gone elsewhere.

During a raid, the wardens would patrol their allotted area, often calling in on people in shelters, and because of their duties, they were often first on the scene after a bomb had landed, often the first to give assistance, be it tackling an incendiary bomb, in a rescue attempt or administering first aid. Wardens were also to act as a guide and give assistance to any person caught out in the street during a raid, directing them to the nearest shelter, to assist those unfortunate to be bombed out of their home and to allay any signs of panic. The warden had to be prepared to be on duty day or night, and those part-time wardens who had regular jobs, had to report for duty at their allotted post on finishing work. If work at bombing incidents carried on past the time they were due to return to their jobs, their duties as a warden took precedence.

A bomb falling at any location within the borough would be first reported by a warden to his own sector warden's post, where it would be passed on to Thornholme, where in one of the rooms large maps of the town adorned the walls and incidents were plotted as and when they were reported. The report from the warden had to be concise and accurate as possible to enable the duty controller to assess which service, fire, ambulance or rescue and demolition, to dispatch to the scene.

Rescue and demolition parties worked at sites where people were known to be trapped in ruins, listening for the slightest sound or movement amongst the rubble, being watchful on where they stepped in case of a collapse of more debris on to other rescuers, those trapped or himself. To tunnel into ruins, leaving a shored-up, safe exit behind, day or night required skill, determination and no small amount of courage, often while a raid was still in progress with the risk of further bombs, unexploded bombs, leaking gas, fires and floods. These squads were controlled by the Borough Engineer.

Following on from the rescuers were the first aid party, which usually consisted of a party of four plus a driver. Red Cross trained men and women had the unenviable task of deciding who was in need of medical attention first,

Stockpiling of gas masks at Monkwearmouth Hospital in 1938.

again, often while bombs were still dropping, and where a mistake could cost valuable time and could be fatal. Later in the war, where possible, a doctor was included in the party.

The ambulance drivers, who were mainly women, often had to negotiate bombed, rubble strewn streets to get the seriously wounded to hospital and those slightly injured to the nearest first aid post. These first aid posts were situated at Commercial Road School, West Park Schools, the Children's Hospital, St Gabriel's Church, the Municipal Hospital and the Royal Infirmary on the south side of the river; and at Monkwearmouth & Southwick Hospital, Old Colliery School, Wheatsheaf, High Southwick Schools, Redby School and Sea Road Schools on the north side of the river. At the first aid post, a doctor, a trained nurse and nursing auxiliaries were on duty. The whole casualty service was under the control of Dr Hebblethwaite, the Medical Officer of Health.

Not all ARP staff had an unblemished record. A post assistant in Roker was dismissed for stealing from her colleagues, while two women, an ambulance driver and an attendant, were dismissed for being absent from duty. A man was dismissed after being found absent from his post at the Cottage Homes and was later found working for a local taxi firm. Another woman, despite being warned many times, was dismissed for entertaining men in the women's quarters.

There were 22 emergency feeding centres, mainly situated in schools, under the control of the Director of Education. These included the Methodist Schoolroom in Dean Terrace, Southwick, the Thompson Memorial Hall in Dundas Street, Wesley Hall in Trimdon Street, Sans Street Mission and Hudson

Casualty Service personnel kitted out for gas attacks, during a exercise at the former Children's Hospital, Durham Road.

Sunderland gas de-contamination unit, November 1939.

Road School. These centres were later supplemented by British Restaurants, which were similar to a factory canteen and where cheap meals were served. The first of these restaurants opened on 10th October 1941 at the South Durham Street unemployed social centre.

Seventeen rest or sleep centres were located in the town where those who were bombed out of their homes were given a bed until alternative billeting arrangements could be made with relatives or friends. Every effort was made to billet homeless as close as possible to their homes. Rest centre accommodation ranged from 40 persons at Cliff Road Presbyterian Church Hall to 370 at West Southwick School. The Women's Volunteer Service, later with the Royal prefix, engaged in a number of tasks from helping at rest centres, handing out clothing to those bombed out to manning mobile canteens. Other sleep centres included Southwick unemployed social centre in Charles Street, Thomas Street North Infants School, Diamond Hall Infants School in Milton Street and Bishopwearmouth C.E. School in Paley Street.

An emergency messenger service of 450 cyclists, consisting mainly of boy scouts was formed. They would have been vital if the phones were rendered inoperable and roads closed to vehicles. The cyclists were dispersed at 130 locations around the town.

If a large scale evacuation of the town was required a fleet of Corporation buses could have been organised. Mobile canteens were based at the Wheatsheaf and Fulwell tram sheds.

Virtually every contingency was planned for and numerous pieces of specialised equipment were kept in readiness at the Northern Region Headquarters, such as a mobile gas cleansing unit, which consisted of a 200 gallon water tank with oil heated boiler, with 6 showers to be used by personnel who had come into contact with poison gas, and hoses for washing contaminated vehicles.

An emergency bath unit, for use in any part of the region where the water supply had been cut off for some time, was fully equipped providing hot water and soap. A mobile washing unit, fitted with washing machines, was manned by volunteers from a local soap making factory.

Military assistance could also be called upon and was greatly appreciated at many incidents in Sunderland. An infantry company, with their own medical officer was available together with a water truck, a signals unit complete with radios and dispatch riders, a section of Military Police and 50 cooks from Catterick Garrison with the facilities to establish field kitchens. The military could also be used to help local farmers fill in bomb craters on their land, providing they paid a rate of $9^1/_2$d (almost 4p) per hour per soldier, with extra for overtime.

Domestic property owners were responsible for their own furniture and belongings if their homes became uninhabitable due to bombing and every assistance was given by rescue squads and wardens. However, there were incidents in Sunderland where members of the Civil Defence were accused of looting at bombing incidents, an example being Suffolk Street in September 1940 where property was reported stolen.

Factories, shipyards and industrial and communication works and buildings which were essential to the war effort were designated Vital Points, and as such were given a code symbol. There were around 34 vital points in Sunderland that would require high priority repair in the event of being damaged in a raid. If damage occurred a warden would report, for example, 8HG1/ONE for Wearmouth Bridge or 8VF4/FOUR for J.L. Thompson's shipyard at North Sands.

Casualty lists were posted as soon as possible after a raid at the Town Hall in Fawcett Street, at the Central Police Station, the Health Offices at Athenaeum Buildings, the Central Library and the Citizens Advice Bureau in Park Terrace.

An air raid shelter being constructed in Mowbray Park, October 1939.

The Mowbray Park shelter, September 1940.

Other shelters included trenches, like these at Southwick Oval, being dug around the time of the Munich Crisis in 1938.

Three mortuaries were located in the town, at Hallgarth Square, Gray Schools in Prospect Row and at J.W. White's Factory.

Plans were made to look after any children orphaned by enemy action, to see if relatives could take them or, if not, the Local Authority.

The ARP animals service was run by two local vets, who would see that any domestic pets had to be taken care of or, if the situation required, destroyed.

All of these services did not materialise overnight, requiring much effort and organisation and even though comprehensive, the ARP services were constantly updated and improved throughout the war. Teams of street fire watchers and office and factory fire guards were established to combat the effectiveness of the incendiary bomb. Armed with a stirrup pump and buckets of sand, almost everyone was required to serve in these roles, and as most were required in action during a raid, a number did lose their lives in Sunderland.

As Britain began to realise that a war with Germany was almost inevitable, preparations took on a more serious outlook during the early months of 1938, a process that accelerated in September due to the Munich Crisis. As Britain was put on an immediate war footing more volunteers were called for to man the ARP.

Among the first acts was to dig trenches for shelter, until more permanent ones could be provided. These included Mowbray Park, the Town Moor, Hendon, West Southwick Oval and in Roker Avenue. On Saturday, 24th September 1938, 22 gas mask fitting centres, mainly situated in schools, opened to hand out and instruct people how to use the masks. These masks had been stockpiled at local schools and hospitals as a measure to reduce fears

A group of wardens pictured in West Sunniside, December 1939.

of chemical warfare. The vision of clouds of poison gas descending over the trenches of France and Flanders during World War One and the agonising deaths and horrific injuries, was still very vivid in the memory. Between 10.00 am and 7.00 pm, 50,000 people were dealt with, but much to many parents' concern there were none of the special baby masks – a situation not fully rectified by the outbreak of war.

As Herr Hitler promised to the then Prime Minister Mr Chamberlain, 'Peace in our time' and the Munich Crisis of September 1938, abated and life returned to some sort of normality, the country was grateful for the chance to expand the ARP so that by the time Hitler annexed Czechoslovakia in the spring of 1939 reneging on the Munich Pact, recruitment and training was well advanced. By the summer of 1939, 2,500 volunteers had enrolled as part-time wardens in the town. However, even after the Munich Crisis, the majority of the populace refused to believe that there would be another war and the ARP service and especially the wardens were regarded with some contempt. Even after war had been declared and the expected deluge of bombs never came, the ARP were seen as people dodging the Armed Forces and generally doing little to support the war effort. This apathetic attitude changed abruptly when the Germans invaded Scandinavia, the Low Countries and France.

Gas masks being issued to children at Commercial Road School.

As the last few months of precious peace gave way to war, the distribution of shelters was started and where it was impractical to put one at each house, a public shelter was provided nearby. The exterior household shelters were of two types. Firstly, the Anderson shelter, was made from sheets of corrugated steel plates bolted together, then set into the ground about 3 feet deep, and then covered with earth. A front entrance was left open to enable a hasty exit and to protect the entrance a blast wall would be built in front. An emergency escape panel was located at the rear. Often these shelters were covered with turf or flowers in an attempt to beautify or conceal. The Ministry of Home Security advised that the earth covering on top of the shelter should be 15 inches thick and 30 inches at the sides.

The Anderson did have its drawbacks as they were prone to flooding and duckboards were essential. Often a drainage system was required, but many a Wearsider owed their lives to the Anderson shelter.

A brick surface shelter was used where households had a backyard and no garden. Similar in size to the Anderson, it had brick walls and a concrete roof and as with the Anderson, could withstand considerable blast.

For indoor use there was the Morrison shelter. This was virtually a oblong box, which served normally as a table, but during a alert, a family would climb inside and meshed panels would be pulled into place at the sides and ends.

Households got into the habit of preparing emergency packs of flasks, torches, cushions and blankets, before retiring to bed. These packs may have gone unused for months then be used for nights in succession.

In the weeks leading up to the conflict it was more or less business as usual in Sunderland, with many Wearsiders enjoying a summer break. News of the test matches with the West Indies and Sunderland football team pre-season preparations ran alongside the Danzig Corridor dispute and Hitler courting friendship with Stalinist Russia.

Gas masks being issued to infants at Commercial Road School.

Left: Anderson shelters being distributed in Ford Estate during March 1939.

Right: An Anderson shelter being 'dug in' at Ford Estate, March 1939.

Left: A well camouflaged and protected Anderson shelter, in Hunter Terrace South, Ford Estate, on the eve of war, August 1939.

War

On Friday, 1st September, Hitler's troops invaded Poland. Full mobilisation was ordered, which included ARP staff and the control rooms were to be manned. A blackout was ordered to take effect that night. Local drapers were hard pressed to supply the heavy duty, light proof curtains. Householders who showed any light through chinks in curtains were threatened with, and occasionally were, prosecuted. It was noted with disgust that some shopkeepers had engaged in unpatriotic profiteering and had put up the prices of their blackout material, brown paper and drawing pins.

Car headlights were fitted with shields, buses and trams had their interior lights dimmed as low as possible and windows half covered with blue paint. Much confusion was caused on the trams by the blacking out of destinations and more than one conductor was reprimanded by irate passengers for the withholding of names of the stops. Any vehicle left unattended had to be immobilised to deny any use to an invader. Again

A young boy, possibly a boy scout, stands guard at a road block in Sunderland.

anyone who didn't follow instructions, including doctors on emergency call, were liable to find themselves in court.

The first night of the blackout did leave a lot to be desired, but following nights brought steady improvement. 'The possibility of lives being jeopardised by the carelessness and ignorance of a minority over this question of lighting control,' commented the Mayor, Coun Myers Wayman, after touring Sunderland on the first night of the blackout. Traders were among the worst offenders for not providing a blackout of their premises. The ARP reckoned that 80 per cent of the town was satisfactorily blacked out. Motorists' experiences suggested that it was only possible to drive safely at speeds of 6-10 mph.

On the night of 2nd September, the Town Hall clock light was extinguished and the chimes silenced.

On that first day of war, the

Bridge Street during the blackout, November 1939. The film was exposed for 4 minutes to achieve this effect.

Sunderland Echo published an 'extra special edition.' Stories of the declaration of war appeared with cricket's Durham Senior League batting averages and the racing results, and the 'Stop Press' mentioned that all Sunderland schools and colleges were to close for at least a week, and parents were urged to watch the *Echo* for announcements regarding evacuation of children.

Parents of children due to be evacuated were advised to prepare clothing. For boys: one vest, one shirt with collar, one pair of underpants, one jersey or pullover, one pair of trousers, handkerchief and two pairs of socks. For girls: one vest or combination, one pair of knickers, one bodice, one petticoat, two pairs of stockings, handkerchiefs, gym slip, blouse, hat and cardigan. Children had to carry night clothes, comb and brush, toothbrush, slippers or sand shoes, towel, soap, face cloth, and if possible an extra pair of boots or shoes. All of these items, plus what the child was wearing, had to have name tags sewn on each item. Parents had to provide a haversack and a holder for their gas mask with shoulder straps and these packs then had to be taken to school at a moment's notice where they were inspected by the headmaster.

The South Hylton Gardening and Industrial Association had to cancel their annual exhibition due to take place that day, while the Sunderland Holiday Fellowship Rambling Club outing to the Alnwick District was also cancelled. Instead, the members were asked to meet in Park Lane to help fill sandbags.

Reaction to the first wartime sounding of the sirens was mixed. Despite the fact that the ARP services had warned that the siren would no longer be sounded, except in the event of an air raid, most people refused to believe that it was anything more than a practice alert. It was reported at the time that it was indeed a false alarm, however a number of unidentified aircraft were seen off the north-east coast flying south. Instead of taking cover, people came out of their homes to chat to neighbours – or to see if this was the envisaged aerial onslaught.

Moments after giving birth to her son John at Highfield Hospital, Jane Stephenson heard the wail of the sirens. A nurse looked into the ward and

Children of Chester Road Schools ready for evacuation, mid-September 1939.

said: 'It's okay Mrs Stephenson, war has just been declared.' Both Jane and her husband, John, were born the year the First World War started, in 1914.

Some trams and buses kept on running instead of stopping to allow passengers to seek shelter. The Mayor was amazed at people's incautious attitude and the fact that some people

Mothers and toddlers arriving at Millfield Station for evacuation, September 1939.

had not yet bothered to obtain their gas masks. On the other hand in the last weeks of peace and the first few of war so many people returned their gas masks to Thornholme for repair or replacement that a charge of 1/6d (7½p) had to be made to help alleviate costs.

The Central and branch libraries, Central Reading Rooms and the Museum and Art Gallery closed at dusk until further notice. Cinemas closed, school children had their holiday break extended, evening church services were cancelled and shops were recommended to close at 6 pm. However, these restrictions were lifted within a few weeks.

Evacuees from Southwick before starting their journey to safety.

As early as 1931, officials planning the defence of the nation were concerned about what effects bombing could have on the population. This led to the government to form the Evacuation Sub-Committee in 1931. However, little planning was undertaken for the mass evacuation of the population until an urgency brought on by the annexation of Austria and the Munich Crisis in 1938. It was proposed that mothers, infants and all school children should be evacuated to safe areas that were less likely to be bombed.

Miss Bright of Chester Road Schools with evacuee twins, Jean and Betty Edmonds and Arthur and Lillian Hepburn, at Northallerton, September 1939.

Initially, Sunderland had not been included in the national evacuation scheme, until protests had been made by local officials and MPs. It wasn't until the declaration of war that the town received full evacuation status. However, plans had been made and the Director of Education, W. Thompson, had been appointed evacuation officer. Any evacuation was voluntary and where possible whole schools were to be evacuated together.

Sunderland's evacuation took place on the 10th September, Newcastle and Gateshead going on the day the Germans invaded Poland (1st September). Almost 8,000 school children left for areas of Durham and North & East Yorkshire. The next day nearly 2,000 mothers and infants left the town. This was less than a third of the town's children.

Many difficulties were experienced which brought a certain amount of frustration, anger and resentment as regards to billeting, education, and the social and class system that existed in Britain at the time together with the fact that there were no bombs dropped in Sunderland for these first few months of the war that it came as little surprise that the evacuation scheme failed. By early 1940 more than half of the evacuees had returned home and by the end of 1942 less than one thousand were still billeted in safe areas.

As early as the 3rd October 1939, the Chairman of the River Wear Commissioners, Alderman F. Nicholson, felt the need to make inquiries regarding the defence of Sunderland docks and harbour installations. These concerns became more urgent when at 1.57 pm, Tuesday 17th October, the sirens sounded in Sunderland, when an aircraft, identified by some as a Heinkel 111, flew over the town without any reaction from the defence forces. Two days later the controller reported to the ARP Committee that in several parts of the town many people failed to hear the sirens. This resulted in increasing the number of sirens sited around Sunderland. The 'all clear' sounded at 3.11 pm.

On the 26th of the month, the Air Ministry returned a rather vague reply stating that: 'Existing deployment would be modified to meet any tactical needs.'

Not surprisingly Alderman F. Nicholson was not put at ease and had become: ' … increasingly alarmed at the apparently defenceless state of Sunderland dock area and shipyards.'

At a meeting at the Town Hall on Friday, 29th March 1940, attended by the Mayor and Alderman Nicholson, it was decided to write to the Regional Commissioner ARP Sir Arthur Lambert, Oliver Stanley at the War Office, Sir Samuel Hoare at the Air Ministry, the First Lord of the Admiralty Winston Churchill and the Controller of Merchant Shipbuilding and Repair Lt-Col Sir James Lithgow. Part of the letter read: 'It is felt very strongly that the docks and river area are insufficiently provided with defensive equipment against the danger of low flying hostile aircraft. There is no barrage balloons at Sunderland and so far as can be ascertained there are scarcely any guns capable of dealing with enemy raiders carrying out a low level attack. It is of course, recognised that, owing to the necessity of secrecy, official information regarding the disposition of batteries for use in the defence of docks and river is not available, but general observation has led to the conclusion that the areas referred to are at present practically defenceless against attack from the air. By way of contrast, general observation gives ground for the belief that the neighbouring River Tyne and its docks have been well provided for with guns for use of driving off raiders, and the Tyne balloon barrage, numbering on occasion 40 balloons, is apparent to all.' The letter went on to describe how vitally important war work was being carried out at Sunderland and that it was estimated that the shipbuilding yards would provide the country with around 100 ships a year. In the absence of any defences and the fact that the yards were concentrated within a small area, it was believed that a determined enemy could do extensive damage to the war effort.

Churchill wrote back, stating that: 'The question of these defences are receiving the immediate attention of the appropriate authorities.'

The reply from the War Office read: 'You may be assured the importance of the Shipbuilding Yards at Sunderland are fully appreciated.'

Looking somewhat uncomfortable, an aircraft spotter of North East Command.

Air Raid Warnings

The various stages of an air raid – Enemy aircraft were located by radar and plotted by the RAF at their headquarters in Newcastle. If an area was thought likely to be attacked, orders for the sirens to be sounded were given to local police stations and the ARP headquarters.

Yellow (Preliminary Caution): issued by phone to a limited number of recipients who take preparatory and unobtrusive measures to be ready to act when Lights Warning or Action Warning is received.

Purple (Lights Warning): A message issued by phone to selected recipients meaning that raiders are expected to pass over the area and immediate action must be take to extinguish all lights required to be extinguished.

Red (Action Warning): Message (on which a public signal will be given) issued by phone to selected recipients meaning that an air raid may occur shortly and that executive action with regard ARP is to be taken.

White (Raiders Passed): Message (if a public signal was be given) issued by phone to all the persons on the lists of Yellow, Purple and Red meaning that raiders have left the area or threat of raid is no longer imminent.

A national air raid warning exercise was held on 31st October 1938. This was followed by numerous local practice alerts such as in Sunderland on 9th August 1939.

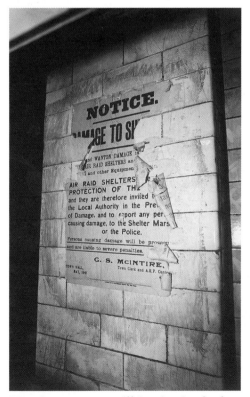

Wartime posters still in situ in the basement of Jessops camera shop, Fawcett Street, which was used as an air raid shelter.

THE FIRST BOMBS
1940

Sunderland Railway Station reopened after being damaged in the raid of 6th September 1940.

Taking advantage of severe winter weather, on the 9th and 11th of January, German aircraft attacked shipping in the North Sea and on Friday the 12th pieces of shrapnel from anti-aircraft shells fell in Southwick, but caused no damage or injuries.

Rationing started on Monday, 8th January, with 4 oz of butter, bacon or ham and 12 oz of sugar allowed per person per week. Further rationing was introduced throughout and after the war including meat, margarine, sweets, cooking fats, clothing, paper and petrol.

On Tuesday, 14th May, 4 days after the Germans had invaded Holland, Belgium and France, the Secretary of State for War, Anthony Eden, broadcast to the Nation announcing the formation of the Local Defence Volunteers, later to be known as the Home Guard. In Sunderland, the first volunteer had signed within 10 minutes of the broadcast. One of the youngest was aged 17 while one of the oldest was 64-year-old James Turnbull of William Street. A veteran of Boer and First World Wars, Mr Turnbull commented: 'I'll serve anywhere as long as it's for England.' By 10.30 am the following day, 125 volunteers had signed up.

On Sunday, 26th May, the Home Secretary authorised that any German or Austrian citizens, between the ages of eighteen and sixty years, were to be temporarily interned. Those living in certain areas, including Durham and Northumberland, had other restrictions imposed such as not using any transport other than public and movements were further restricted by a curfew from 8 pm to 6 am.

Another announcement, this time from the Minister of Health, said: 'The Government has decided that all aliens employed in public utility undertakings, should, unless their credentials are unexceptionable, be regarded

Glass bottles being stored, possibly by Local Defence Volunteers or Home Guard, to be used as petrol bombs in the event of an invasion.

Home Guard anti-parachutists unit in Sunderland, 1940.

as a potential danger and be eliminated from positions of trust or positions in which damage might be done.'

Two days later, from the cleansing department came letters about 2 employees, a street sweeper of 'very doubtful antecedants and a very advanced communist,' and a binman of 'reputed Italian extraction and of communistic propensities.'

It was also noted that there were a doctor and a number of nurses born in the Irish Free State (the IRA were active on the U.K. mainland at this time) and two nurses of German nationality employed at the Municipal Hospital.

The *Sunderland Echo* later reported that five aliens had been arrested and interned and a further 300 were subject to stringent supervision on Wearside.

The end of May 1940 saw the German army closing in on the British Expeditionary Force trapped at Dunkirk. The mood was indeed gloomy and an indication of how desperate the situation was becoming can possibly be gauged from a message, received by the Town Clerk, from the regional commissioner, for his personal and private information. The message read:

31/5/40
SECRET. IT IS CONSIDERED BY THE CHIEFS OF STAFF THAT AN ATTACK ON THIS COUNTRY IS IMMINENT. ENEMY MAY USE LARGE FLEETS OF FAST MOTOR BOATS SIMULTANEOUS WITH AIRBORNE RAIDS INLAND. MILITARY COMMANDERS HAVE BEEN WARNED.
ACKNOWLEDGE.

From Monday, 10th June road signs were ordered removed, as the threat of invasion became more and more likely and 3 days later the ringing of church bells was banned except as a signal of invasion.

On Wednesday, 19th June, just a few days before the first bombs fell in the area, the *Sunderland Echo* published figures relating to ARP manpower shortages in Sunderland. Over 2,800 vacancies needed to be filled, broken down into 906 wardens, 819 casualty service including ambulancemen, 550 rescue and demolition, 395 AFS and decontamination 155.

First Bombs

The first bombs dropped on the Sunderland district fell soon after midnight on Saturday 22nd, June. The sirens had sounded at around 11.32 pm Friday 21st, (The all clear sounded at 1.50 am. The sirens sounded again at 3.36 am and the all clear at 3.58am)and soon afterwards a single aircraft was heard flying from the direction of the sea. The aircraft flew inland for only a few miles before retracing its steps, flying over Whitburn. Just before recrossing the coast, it released three High Explosive (HE) bombs.

The first fell into a field adjoining the Old Rectory in Whitburn, demolishing a centuries-old tithe barn, killing a horse, or horses, stabled there. The unfortunate beast, or beasts, ended up buried in the resulting crater. The second bomb fell on the field path from Church Lane to The Bents and the third narrowly missed the Fishermen's Cottages. Most of the people living in the cottages had taken to their Anderson shelters and all later gave praise as to their effectiveness. Thomas Betts, who said: 'The explosion was terrific,' was with his daughter, Ellen, only 15 yards from the crater. The Bryan family took what cover they could under the stairs, while Cuthbert Hutchinson remained in the kitchen of his cottage and stood up against a wall, but was shocked when part of the ceiling fell in and the outer door was blown past him to knock down an inner door.

A number of incendiary bombs fell on the main coast road near to the Cottages, but caused no damage and quickly burned themselves out. The craters drew curious onlookers for many days afterwards to view the first bomb damage.

As alerts became more frequent, it was noted by the authorities that large

The first bombs fall close to the Fishermen's Cottages at The Bents, 22nd June 1940.

groups of people were going to shelters in many parts of the town at around 11.00 pm and demanding that the shelters be opened even though no alert had sounded. The authorities advised the public that shelters would be opened only on the sirens sounding and to go to public shelters only if they had no shelter of their own.

The Germans lost an aircraft close to Sunderland at 11.55 pm, Friday, 19th July. A Focke Wulf 200C-1 'Condor' was caught in searchlight beams off the coast between Sunderland and Hartlepool. The aircraft had set out from Marx, France, on a minelaying operation and had flown too close to the shore and despite trying desperately to avoid the searchlights the 'Condor' was engaged and shot down by anti-aircraft fire. Part of the

One of the Cottage residents with an unexploded incendiary bomb.

undercarriage from this aircraft was picked up a number of years ago in a fishing boat's nets and is now on display at the North East Aircraft Museum.

The Luftwaffe's next visit was again nocturnal, during the early hours of Sunday, 21st July.

At 1.45 am, farmer George Reed and his wife were rudely awoken by the sound of a huge explosion, which violently shook their house at Witherwack Farm. Going outside, Mr Reed heard the aircraft apparently going in a westerly direction over the farm, with searchlights trying in vain to catch the bomber in their beams. Mr Reed claimed that: 'He was flying so low that I could have brought him down with my rifle.'

The crater, found at daybreak by a farmhand, revealed the bomb had fallen on a hedge between grass land and a turnip field, 60 yards east of the farm buildings, and 12 yards from a piggery. Windows in the farmhouse and piggery were shattered and 2 farm carts were wrecked.

An incendiary bomb fell into Hylton Dene, or Swallow Dene, 50 yards inside the Borough boundary, 100 yards from Hylton Colliery, Castletown. Police from Sunderland and Durham County argued as to whether the bomb had actually fell inside the Borough.

During the night of 23rd/24th July, enemy aircraft were again operating just off the coast near Sunderland. Searchlight batteries near to the sea reported 3 HE bombs falling into the sea, just off the shoreline. Often coastguards along the Durham coast could see aircraft avoiding searchlights, laying mines which occasionally paid dividends for the Germans.

On Friday, 26th July, the SS *Balzac* was lying at anchor off the piers at around 9.30 pm when the ship was rocked by an explosion. Within 10 minutes, casualties were being ferried to Sunderland's Corporation Quay. Those admitted to the Royal Infirmary included nine Norwegian sailors and two British gunners, all but two of the sailors suffered from the effects of being in the sea and one sailor had broken limbs and a stomach wound. The SS *Bazac* had left Sunderland docks at 8.00 pm to join a convoy.

First Casualties

Air raids on the north-east were not such a large affair, yet, where more usually only one or two aircraft were involved. Friday, 9th August, saw Sunderland's first air raid casualties of the war.

'Raid 10' was plotted at the sector operations room at RAF Usworth at 11.16 am, 45 miles east of the Farne Islands, heading south-west towards Blyth. The German aircraft crossed the coast at South Shields, passing north-east of Usworth and re-crossed the coast at Sunderland. 'Yellow' section 79 Sqdn were scrambled from Acklington, Northumberland, at 11.22 am and instructed to intercept the raider.

The 'Yellow' alert was received late in the morning at 11.35 am, and 10 minutes later bombs were heard exploding on the north side of the river. It was soon reported that bombs had fallen on railway installations and other properties on the riverside.

The bomber, a Heinkel He111 was reportedly on an armed reconnaissance mission to Scotland. However, the aircraft was caught over the town by 3 Hurricanes of 79 Sqdn. (Flown by Fl-Lt Rupert Francis Henry Clereke, PO George Hassall 'Neddy' Nelson-Edwards and Sgt John Wright.) Whether the German crew dumped their bombs in order to aid their escape, or carried out a bombing run will probably never be known. Whatever the case, 14 bombs fell causing considerable damage.

Of the bombs that fell, the most serious were those that fell in Laing's shipyard, and it was here that the first fatalities occurred, when Arthur Perry, Richard Archer, Thompson Reed and P. Sloan died of injuries they received. In

Four men were killed at Laing's shipyard, during a lunchtime raid by a single aircraft 9th August 1940.

all, 5 bombs fell in the shipyard, fortunately only 2 exploded. One fell next to the frame bending furnace and loft steps, blowing over a steam traction engine which had just delivered steel plates. Other damage included the plasterer's shed roof and a hydraulic crane arm that was broken off. Another bomb scored a direct hit on the yard's air raid shelter, but as the sirens had not sounded the shelter was empty. The uxb's were cordened off and a LDV (Home Guard) guard was posted to keep the inquisative away. One uxb, at Ayre's Quay glassworks, was not found and dealt with until October 1942.

A direct hit on the Sheepfolds railway bridge put out of use the north bound line of the London & North Eastern Railway. Single line working was put into operation. It was initially reported to 'Thornholme' that the railway company hoped to have the line repaired within 6 hours. It was somewhat fortunate that the bomb had not been of a larger calibre as to demolish the bridge, which would have had caused chaos to rail traffic. Buildings around the bridge, including the Royal Hotel, were blast damaged.

The railway bridge at the Sheepfolds, next to Monkwearmouth Station, damaged by a direct hit.

Inside the Royal Hotel, the proprietor, Victor Seaton, standing at the top of the cellar steps, was blown down the steps into the cellar, while their housekeeper, Charlotte Sawkill, sustained severe chest injuries when a window she was standing next to blew in.

Caught in the open during the bombing was Irene Mooney (20), of Richmond Street, Monkwearmouth. Initial reports claimed she had a broken leg, but Irene's injuries must have been more severe as she succumbed to her injuries at Monkwearmouth & Southwick Hospital on 13th August.

Close to the Royal Hotel were lorry driver William Berkley and his 17-year-old assistant

The Royal Hotel, next to the bridge with the windows blown in.

Stanley Monk. They were only yards from where the bomb exploded, but both had a lucky escape, as blast and debris wrenched a door off their cab, Berkley emerging with cuts and a broken leg and Monk was unscathed.

Annie Conlon (22), of Woodyer Terrace, suffered from shock and abrasions from being hurled to the ground by blast from one of the bombs.

A bomb fell on the gents lavatory situated on the corner of Sheepfolds and Hay Street, damaging the LNER offices situated in Monkwearmouth Goods yard.

Two bombs fell in Back Bonnersfield, damaging houses. A direct hit on the Ali Baba Sauce factory practically demolished the building. Five factory girls, May Alice Alderson (15), E. Bell (15), Irene Patterson (16), Eileen Fail (15) and Lilian Mason (16) were treated for shock. Another bomb fell in the river near to Austin's pontoon and others in Wreath Quay Road and Wreath Quay Lane. The Aerocrete Works in Stoney Lane suffered a direct hit, but the bomb failed to explode.

Any elation the German crew might have felt in hitting the shipyards and a bridge, if in fact they knew, was short lived, as they were forced to ditch their aircraft into the sea about a mile off Whitburn. Many people in the Roker area caught glimpses of the German bomber and RAF Hurricanes between the clouds and the sound of machine gun fire was clearly audible. After alighting on the sea the crew managed to escape to their dinghy and were picked up by Royal Navy patrol boat. One can wonder at the thoughts of Willi Haertel and Otto Denner, Gustav Karkos and Fritz Feinekat as they were landed at Corporation Quay, well within sight of their handiwork. They were met by two RAF officers and a military guard from the 2nd/4th Essex Regiment, two being taken to Dykelands Road Drill Hall in Seaburn, the two wounded, Karkos and Feinekat, to the Royal Infirmary.

Just 2 days later, on Monday, 12th August, the Luftwaffe were back, as at 11.38 pm air raid warning 'Red' was received and the sirens sounded. The aircraft plotted was possibly 'raid 6' which appeared from the north-east at a height of 7,000 feet and remained off Sunderland at heights varying from 3,000 to 20,000 feet. At 00.45 am, 3 bombs fell, 1 to the north end of east Back Parade, Hendon, the second outside the entrance to the Monsanto Chemical Works situated at the south end of Hendon Docks and the third at the East Quay of Hendon Dock.

In Back Parade the bomb demolished the outhouses of 6 houses which were also seriously damaged. From 79 The Parade, Florence Semple and her children George (8) and Helga (2) were dug out from the ruins of their home and treated at Commercial Road first aid post.

Four small fires were quickly extinguished in the damaged houses.

At the premises of John Robson Ltd, ship ventilator maker, situated at the east side of Back Parade, damage was considerable, with gas and water mains burst, and overhead telephone wires needing repair.

The bomb at the Monsanto Chemical Works (or National Benzole & British Oil Storage) caused blast damage to a gable end of a building and tore up railway lines, hurling a piece of track 30 feet in length, over a 12 feet high wall, which on landing severed a chemical pipeline.

The bomb on the east side of Hendon Dock fell between 2 sets of railway lines. Both railway lines were torn up for a distance of 40 yards, 2 railway wagons were overturned and damaged.

In all, 10 people from The Parade and 2 from the docks were treated for minor injuries. One of those injured was warden John Day (37), who was treated for cuts on his scalp and bruises to his temple and legs. The all clear was sounded at 1.06 am 13th August, and again after a 'yellow' alert at 4.06 am.

In 2 successive raids the Germans had managed to hit and damage

Back Parade, Hendon, damaged during a raid on 12th August.

industrial or legitimate targets in Sunderland.

By mid-August, the Luftwaffe High Command believed that the RAF fighter squadrons were in a weak state. Poor intelligence-gathering had left the Germans in total ignorance as to how the RAF fighter control system operated. Even though the main action was taking place in southern England, it was deemed prudent to keep a minimum force in quieter sectors of the country. Often these forces were squadrons which had been in action and were resting, replacing losses, but still had a nucleus of battle experienced pilots to train new-comers.

The Luftwaffe decided that the knock-out blow should be an all-out attack around the country, the usual raids in the south together with a raid launched from Norway. towards the north-east coast. Their targets were thought to be airfields in North Yorkshire with secondary targets being Middlesbrough.

From the outset things went badly for the Germans. A feint attack to the Firth of Forth by seaplanes, Heinkel He115's, was, due to a navigation error, almost exactly followed by Heinkel He 111's and their escort of Messerschmitt Bf110D's.

Around noon, radar stations in Scotland and Northumberland began to pick up the first plots of a force of about 20-plus aircraft, some 90 miles off the Firth of Forth. At 13 Group Headquarters, in Blakelaw, Newcastle, the north-east's first big daylight raid was watched with interest. By now navigators in the German formation had realised their error and had altered course and were now heading for Tyneside. As the Germans neared land the estimation of size of the formation increased to 30 plus, and at 12.10 pm the fighter controller scrambled 72 Sqdn's 12 Spitfires from Acklington, putting them on an intercept course to meet near the Farne Islands. Soon afterwards two flights of 605 Sqdn's Hurricanes based at Drem in Scotland were scrambled and 79 Sqdn at Acklington were ordered to readiness.

East of the Farne Islands, 72 Sqdn, led by Fl-Lt Ted Graham caught sight of the raiders and were surprised to find not 30-plus but around 100 enemy aircraft!

Using the extra 3,000 feet of height the Spitfires had gained, Graham led his pilots down through the escorting fighters and on to the bombers. Within seconds the German fighters had lost their leader, his aircraft apparently exploding when bullets ignited the petrol gases in the 'dachshund' belly fuel tank. A number of the bombers jettisoned their bombs.

72 Sqdn's attack broke up the German formation into 2 groups. Hurricanes of 79 Sqdn and the Usworth based 607 Sqdn 'County of Durham', were ordered into action as were the Spitfires of 41 Sqdn from Catterick. By this time the raiders were over the Tynemouth area and approaching Sunderland. In the town, many people were returning to work after their lunch break when the sirens sounded at 12.50 pm, and those in the ARP services had to quickly return home to take up their duties.

The sound of gunfire could be heard towards the north, and the roar of aero engines was growing in intensity. Through gaps in the clouds diamond formations of aircraft could be seen, many people taking them to be British aircraft and were standing out in the open. A man and his son who were swimming near to the Cat & Dog Steps had an excellent, albeit dangerous, view of the air battle unfolding above them.

The Germans, one group over the coast, the other over the Greyhound Stadium were still flying south and now the anti-aircraft guns around the town took up the challenge. Another noise, that of exploding bombs, soon followed. All but one of the bombs fell in Fulwell area.

At 1 Eston Grove a bomb fell in the front garden, bursting a gas main, causing considerable damage to the house. The occupants, in their shelter, were uninjured.

In Viewforth Terrace, bombs fell at Nos 6 and 8, where the bomb landed on the offshot in the yard, causing extensive damage to both houses. At Nos 10 and 12, a direct hit demolished the house. Warden Edward Smith was in his shelter in Atkinson Road, when he heard the scream of the bombs falling and the detonations.

He immediately left for the scene, and while the raid was still in progress, went to see what assistance he could give. Finding No 10 badly damaged and knowing that a Mrs Jackson and another lady were inside, he began to clear away debris to rescue both women, one of whom had a broken arm. Within seconds of pulling the women clear, the roof and upper floor collapsed on to the spot from where the women were rescued.

In a letter to the ARP controller, Group 7 deputy head warden R. Harrison wrote: 'By his (Smith's)

Numbers 8 and 10 Viewforth Terrace, Fulwell.

prompt action and complete disregard for his own safety, he undoubtedly saved the women from severe injury, if not death.'

At No 27, another semi-detached house was demolished by a direct hit, but the adjoining house was undamaged, one of those strange occurrences that happened during bombing.

At 20 Charlton Road, a crater in the front garden burst a water main, shattered windows and caused damage to the roof. The only person in the house was 69-year-old Margaret Coleman, who was totally deaf and was blissfully unaware that anything had happened.

Sheltering underneath the dining room table at 12 Thompson Road were a woman and her daughters aged 16, 18 and 24, when bombs fell to the front and rear of the house. They all escaped injury and the house was only slightly damaged, but an unfinished surface shelter was demolished.

Another close escape was for those sheltering in the front garden of 3 Thompson Road, when a bomb exploded only 3 yards from both shelter and house. A man and 4 women in the shelter were uninjured, the roof, dining room walls and kitchen ceiling had collapsed. A garage in the garden was blown on its end and a car inside with it.

At 32 Grange View, fortune was with those sheltering in a concrete shelter built into the ground. A bomb landed so close to the shelter that part of the wall collapsed, but the 4 women, 2 men and 3 children, aged between 3 and and 10 years old, emerged unhurt, though not surprisingly, in a state of shock.

Another bomb exploded by the side of 60 Wearmouth Drive, occupied by PC Thomas Gaundry, which demolished the whole side of the house, Mrs Gaundry emerged from their Anderson shelter suffering from shock. Next door at No 62, occupied by James Scott, a piece of concrete 1 ft square by 4 inches thick smashed through the roof and a number of walls in the house were cracked

60 Wearmouth Drive.

while on the other side at No 58, were Mrs Phillips and her two children: 'I thought our end had come when I heard the bombers overhead. My two kiddies began to scream and I clutched them beneath me as I felt the shelter rock under the blast.'

Further down the street, at No 48, a bomb landed in the back garden causing cracks in the walls in every room in the house, but windows only eight yards from the crater were unbroken.

At 1 Melvyn Gardens a bomb burst a water main and at No 11, occupied by another policeman, PC H. Coates, a bomb demolished his house. His wife and child were in their Anderson shelter which was covered in debris, but both were unhurt.

Pensioners Mr & Mrs Ferens, of 15 Johanna Street, escaped serious injury by sheltering under the stairs. A bomb had apparently come through the roof, the staircase was virtualy the only intact part of the demolished house.

15 Johanna Street, where an elderly couple were lucky to escape injury.

In Atkinson Road, 40 and 48 received direct hits demolishing both.

Taking refuge in his shop doorway at 40 Sea Road, were master butcher and part-time warden Thomas Jones, and warden John Skillett (54). A bomb landed on Kemp's Store directly opposite the butcher's shop, seriously wounding Skillett, his left arm was almost severed. Despite severe lacerations and a suspected fractured ankle, Jones struggled into his shop and telephoned a concise report to the centre in Dene Lane. Jones then returned to the profusely bleeding Skillett, and applied a tourniquet to his shattered arm with his haversack strap. A first aid party from Redby casualty depot, took both

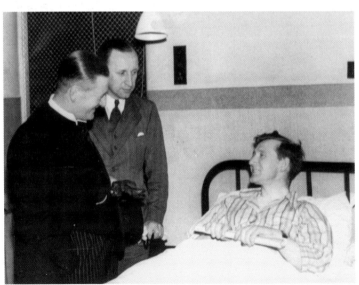

The Mayor and Town Clerk visit Warden Thomas Jones in hospital.

men to the Monkwearmouth and Southwick Hospital, where Skillett's arm was amputated and Jones' wounds treated.

In a letter to the chairman and members of the War Emergency Committee, dated 20th August, Chief Constable Cook stated that warden Jones' actions: 'Most probably saved warden Skillett's life' and considered: 'His (Jones') actions most meritorious and deserving of the highest commendation.'

Luck or fortune was not with everyone that August afternoon. At Eden House, in Eden Place just off Newcastle Road, Doris Jobling (26), George Todd (27) and Elsie Holt (14) were in the kitchen when a bomb struck the building, killing them. Warden John Henderson (29), who was on his first day of duty, was also killed when caught in the blast of one of the bombs.

Bombs fell at a number of other locations, causing damage to varying degrees. In Grasmere Crescent, Denbigh Avenue, Moine Gardens, Park Lea Road, Elizabeth Street, William Street and Neale Street, houses were damaged by near misses. In Annie Street, 5 houses were demolished and 17 houses were badly damaged in Zion Terrace.

The single bomb to land on the south side of the river, landed in High Street East, a drug store owned by George Bell. The shop was extensivly damaged and a house in Low Street, directly behind the shop was damaged. Warden Albert Gibbons, reported a uxb in the river, close to the fish quay 40 yards from the rear of the drug store.

Uxb's fell in Dene Lane, at 75 Side Cliffe Road, the Grange Hotel yard, Denbigh Avenue, on Binns recreation ground, 2 in Mere Knolls Cemetery near to the Lodge, 2 in Tyzack's Yard in Fulwell Road and in the quarry near to the anti-aircraft gun positions.

ARP Regional Commissioner Sir Arthur Lambert with the Mayor Councillor Myers Wayman and other officials tour the damaged streets in Fulwell, in this case Newcastle Road, 15th August 1940.

As an indication of the damage that could be caused by a HE bomb, in Sea Road only one bomb fell, that on Kemp's Store at No 59. On the same side of the road odd Nos 31 to 101 and even Nos 22 to 58 all received damage.

The all clear sounded at 2.10 pm.

The German aircraft had been harried virtually non-stop since 72 Sqdn. had made the initial interception near to the Farne Islands. To the Luftwaffe crews, some with dead and wounded onboard their damaged aircraft, limping home to their bases in Norway, the day would be forever known as 'Der Schwarzer Donnerstag' - Black Thursday. From the north-east raid, a later raid on the airfields in Yorkshire and raids on the south coast, a total of 75 Luftwaffe aircraft were shot down, more than on the day we now celebrate as Battle of Britain day, September 15th, when the Germans lost 56 aircraft.

The raid cost the Germans 8 Heinkels 111 bombers and 6 Messerschmitt Bf 110 fighters. Reflecting on these losses the Luftwaffe High Command decided that North-East England was no place for large bomber formations in daylight.

On the 23rd August, Observer Corps reported that an aircraft crashed into the sea off Seaburn at 1.28 am. No wreckage was found despite confirmation of the crash coming from the searchlight site at Cleadon, the gun site at Whitburn and the military on the coast.

The town's next brush with the Luftwaffe came during the night and early morning of 26th/27th August, when a single raider was heard, for some minutes, flying low over the blacked out town. Small by comparison with the 15th August raid, it was, however, the longest alert so far from 10.15 pm to 3.37 am.

At 1.50 am, those on duty at Police Headquarters heard bombs exploding. Reports soon indicated that bombs had fallen near Seaburn railway station and near to the junction of Queen Alexandra Road and Silksworth Lane. Ten bombs fell, 9 of which exploded, the uxb was found at the south end of Marina Avenue, Fulwell.

At 'Hilldene,' 2 Seaforth Road, a HE bomb landed in the garden, demolishing the house. At first the authorities believed that the occupiers, Arthur (64) and Margaret Taylor (66) were sheltering at the nearby water works in Seaforth Road, but in a letter to the Town Clerk, dated 23rd September, 1940, Miss Hilda Lisle (27) stated that she and her 60-year-old mother, also named Hilda, were sheltering under the stairs, with the Taylors in 'Hilldene.' All were in a state of shock when they extricated themselves from the ruins and Mrs Taylor had been cut on the cheek by flying glass. The Lisle's home at 30 Humbledon Park was also badly damaged.

2 Seaforth Road, Humbledon.

Miss Lisle went to describe their horror on emerging from 'Hilldene' to see the house opposite, named 'Hill House,' had also been badly damaged and that lights could be seen from blown out doors and windows. Despite not being a 'young man and not enjoying the best of health for some time', Mr Taylor rushed into the house, not knowing where the bomb had fallen and oblivious to the danger of falling

8 Huntingdon Gardens, Humbledon.

masonry. He was unable to find the light switches so removed the bulbs from their sockets in case the light attracted further bombers. For his actions, Mr Taylor was sent a letter of commendation from the Town Clerk.

Mrs M.P. Thompson in 'Hill House,' where the bomb had burst, was more upset at the destruction of her apple orchard, some of the apples being blown into the grounds of the Children's Hospital: 'We were sitting in a room when we heard the bombs starting and made a dive for the cupboard under the stairs. We had barely got in - there wasn't time to close the door - before there was a blinding flash and the house seemed to be coming down around our ears. The next I remember was shouting for a warden and then I woke up in hospital.'

In a house close to the Children's Hospital Mr and Mrs Elsy and their young son hid under a bed with a piano pulled in front for extra protection, but all escaped injury when one wall was blown in and the piano wrecked.

Bombs also fell at 29 and 30 Humbledon Park, 8, 9 or 10 Huntingdon Gardens, 16, 17, 18 Hillfield Gardens and in Silksworth Lane, where Seadons Workshop was demolished. A further 100 or so houses received damage and gas and water supplies were affected. Overhead electric tram wires in Durham Road were severed.

Across the River Wear, on duty in Fulwell Road, was Inspector Donald. At 2.00 am he heard an aircraft overhead, soon followed by loud explosions. Windows in Fulwell Road were blown in. Two bombs had exploded, in Prince George Avenue and Marina Avenue, where there was also an uxb. After reporting to Dene Lane ARP centre, Donald went to Prince George Avenue arriving at the same time as the rescue & demolition squad No 4 led by staff officer William Joss, who quickly sealed a burst water pipe, checked damaged buildings and said they would return at first light to deal with a wall in danger of collapsing at No 18.

At No 18, Albert Elliott and his wife were in their shelter when a bomb landed close by: 'After a smaller bomb had landed nearby I heard the "screamer" coming down. It was a horrible moment. I knew it was going to hit my house. There was a tremendous explosion but the shelter stayed put.'

Next door at No 16 lived George Stoddart. He and his wife had not returned home after the sirens had sounded and it was probably fortunate they hadn't as the Stoddarts returned home to find their house demolished.

Another house opposite that of Mr Elliott's was badly damaged, the elderly couple who owned it had left the previous day for a short holiday. However, their shelter was used by two other families and when the bombs fell a piece of shrapnel went through the back wall of the shelter without injuring anyone.

18 Prince George Avenue, Fulwell, destroyed during a raid on the 27th August.

Nearby Miss Elsie Greenwell was having a nightmare in which she was in an air raid when she was rudely woken by: 'A most appalling crash.' A piece of shrapnel had drilled through the brickwork, through an easy chair and into a piano.

Also close to the explosion were Mrs Greivson and her sons, who escaped unhurt from their shelter even though a door had been blown off its hinges and smashed to pieces and the shelter being lifted out of the ground.

Warden Harry Myers was on duty about a 100 yards from his house when it was wrecked in a explosion, his wife being in their Anderson shelter only 5 yards from the crater, escaped with shock.

The only casualty was a Mrs Barker of No 14 who suffered from shock and a sprained ankle. A nurse who was passing at the time was called in to treat her.

By now the all clear had sounded, and all those emerging from their shelters, living close to the uxb bomb or whose homes were untenable, were evacuated to family and friends around the town.

The next raid on the town, during the night and early morning of Thursday/Friday 5th/6th September, is arguably the best-known, as it saw the demise of one of the raiders over the heart of the town, but with tragic consequences.

Flying from their base in Soesteberg, Holland, were Hans-Werner Schroder, Franz Reitz, Rudolf Marten and Josef Wich in a Heinkel He111P. Around 11.15 pm the aircraft crossed the coast at Sunderland and was immediately caught in searchlight beams. Anti-aircraft gunners soon found the range. Eye-witnesses described a shell bursting close to the tail of the aircraft, the note of the engines changing abruptly. A shower of rockets or flares came from the plane followed by dense smoke. Watching crowds cheered as the plane was hit.

Sheltering in their brick surface shelter at their home at 55$^1/_2$ Suffolk Street were John and Rachel Stormont (41) and their 15-year-old daughter Jean, who had recently started work at the post office and was hoping to train as a telephonist. At 11.18pm her life was cruelly torn apart when the carcass of the stricken Heinkel crashed on to her house and shelter, the petrol from the wing

The wheels of the Heinkel bomber that crashed in Suffolk Street.

tanks exploding into flames.

Fire Brigade Superintendent T. Bruce, was dispatched to Suffolk Street from the Hendon auxiliary fire station with 2 tenders, additional foam apparatus and 3 auxiliary fire pumps. The Heinkel had destroyed a shop and a house and had badly damaged 2 other houses, and fires were burning furiously at front and rear of the building.

The Stormonts were trapped in their blazing shelter, which was covered in debris from buildings and aircraft. Supt. Bruce and Fire Sergeant Patterson were assisted by Chief Inspector Middlemist, Detective G. Cook, and Detective Constables Buddles and Simpson, in removing slabs of concrete and other debris from the shelter and managed to rescue the Stormonts. During the rescue a jet of water had to be played onto the feet of the trapped family which were being burned.

Rachael Stormont was found to be dead when brought from the shelter, John and Jean both seriously injured.

Supt. Bruce later summed up in his report: 'All the rescuers displayed exceptional courage as rescue operations were greatly hampered by the flames and heat given off by the burning petrol and in addition concentrations of

ARP workers clearing the site of the bomber crash in Suffolk Street.

petrol vapour exploding continuously. The men showed complete disregard to the fact further bombs may have been in the fallen plane and could have exploded at any time during the operations.'

Jean's injuries were such that her hands had to be amputated and she had a serious leg injury. She spent 2 years in hospital recovering and learning to use her artificial hands. Fearing that her career as a telephonist was over before it had started, in June, 1943 she began work with limbs that were specially adapted for her to use the switchboard. Jean's father, a shipyard plumber, recovered from his injuries and had returned to work.

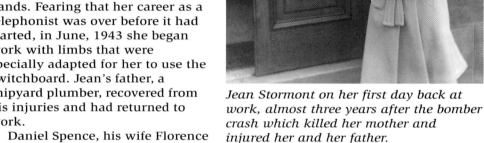

Jean Stormont on her first day back at work, almost three years after the bomber crash which killed her mother and injured her and her father.

Daniel Spence, his wife Florence and daughter Joan (16) were in bed when the plane crashed. Going downstairs they found their kitchen a mass of flames, but managed to get out through a shattered shop front.

Bombs from the crashed plane littered the surrounding streets. Two in South Back Athol Road, at Nos 35, 36 and at 39 Athol Road, at 42 and 46 Robinson

Some of the residents made homeless by the bomber crash, wait to be billeted with family or friends.

Street and 2 at 25 Hendon Burn Avenue all of which failed to detonate. One bomb did explode, between 2 and 3 Ward Street, severely damaging both houses and slightly injuring Annie Lamb and her 12-year-old daughter Isabella at No 2.

During the raid, William and Gladys Collins were in their shelter at 7 Villette Brooke Street. They heard the aircraft losing height rapidly, making a terrible whining, screaming noise and a huge explosion when it finally came to earth. Leaving their shelter, after the all clear, and still in total darkness, Mrs Collins saw an object in the yard giving off luminous light. Upon investigation it was found to be the altimeter, which had frozen at the height the bomber was hit. The Collins's decided to keep the device as a souvenir, but after repeated days of intensive public appeals by the ARP and police, it was handed in.

Other pieces of wreckage, maps and equipment were found in various other places around the town.

All the German airmen were killed. Twenty-seven-year-old Rudolf Marten and Josef Wich (25) crashed to earth in their disintegrating aircraft. Franz Reitz (24) was found with opened parachute on the roof of the public air raid shelter at Bede Towers in Ryhope Road, with horrific head injuries. The body of the officer Hans-Werner Schroder (27) was found not far from his comrade, in the front garden of 5 Grange Crescent, his parachute unopened, again with severe head injuries. It is not known if these men managed to jump, fell or were blown from their stricken plane. The bodies were taken to Low Street mortuary, where clothing and equipment were removed and handed to an RAF intelligence officer from 13 Group headquarters. At least 3 of the airmen had been awarded the Iron Cross, suggesting they had seen some previous action, and all were buried with military honours by the RAF at Castletown cemetery where they remain to this day.

During work for the construction of the Health Centre in Suffolk Street in 1986, a complete engine from the Heinkel was unearthed and was

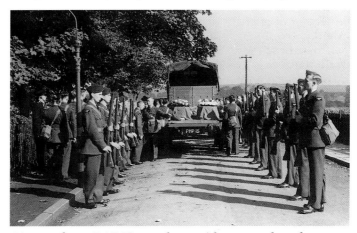

Airmen from RAF Usworth provide a guard at the funeral of the German airmen at Hylton Cemetery.

Airmen fire a salute above the graves of the bomber crew.

given to the North East Aircraft Museum.

Two hours later at 1.13 am Friday, 6th September, another enemy bomber flew over the town. This crew had considerably more success than their earlier comrades, dropping a number of bombs around the railway station and town centre.

A large bomb crashed through the roof of the central railway station and exploded on the platform, causing extensive damage. A carriage was blown off the rails and on to the platform. A girder 10 feet by 4 inches was blown 200 yards and landed in Northumberland Street and 4 carriage wheels were blown through the roof and came to rest in Joseph's toy and sports shop window in Union Street.

On duty at the Suffolk Street incident was warden M.I. Joseph, who recalled in a letter to the *Sunderland Echo* in 1989, that fire chief Bruce had advised Mr Joseph to return to his shop as carriage wheels were in his shop window. At daylight after assessing the damage, Mr Joseph asked the LNER to remove the wheels, who refused claiming that: 'They did not put them there.' Eventually the Borough Council removed the wheels, but this prompted an argument between council

Sunderland Railway Station damaged by a direct hit.

Sunderland Station exterior. Carriage wheels came over the wall close to where the men are standing.

Warden Monty Joseph examines the railway bogey wheels blasted into his shop front from Sunderland Station.

officers and LNER over the scrap rights to the wheels.

A second bomb fell between the station and the back of Fawcett Street, damaging a gas main near to the Town Hall and the Sunderland Working Men's Building Society. The shelter for the Town Hall staff was partially buried in the bomb crater, but the shelter was empty at the time. The public reading room was damaged, but opened as usual later that morning. However, in the interests of safety it was later closed for repair.

Large numbers of incendiary bombs fell behind the Regal Cinema in Holmeside, near the Stockton Road railway bridge, on the embankment between Stockton Road and Tunstall Road and in the grounds of 'Somerlayton' in Thornhill Terrace. All these bombs caused small fires that were quickly extinguished. One railway employee was injured.

As the town braced itself for its next visit from the Luftwaffe, and with the probability of the raids increasing in both size and frequency, many parents again turned their thoughts to the evacuation of their children to safer areas of the country or even abroad.

The Luftwaffe bombers were back over Sunderland on Thursday, 10th October, the sirens sounding at 7.55 pm, the all clear 2 hours later.

Station Street bomb damage.

City of Benares

On Tuesday, 17th September, the liner *City of Benares*, carrying 89 evacuees, including a dozen from Sunderland, was hundreds of miles from land in the Atlantic Ocean, destination Canada. Around 10.00 pm, *City of Benares* was torpedoed by a U-Boat, in total darkness and in heavy seas. Of the 89 evacuees, 12 survived, which included only two of the Sunderland children.

This U-Boat attack took place without warning, in rough seas and in total darkness and of the 429 passengers and crew 279 lost their lives. The attack caused a wave of indignation throughout the then neutral United States of America. It also wasn't the first time that an evacuee ship had been sunk. Another liner had been torpedoed off the west coast of Ireland, again in darkness and rough seas, but on this occasion there were no casualties. There were two Sunderland evacuees on board, Frank (13) and Hubert (11) Entwisle, sons of Pastor Hubert Entwisle of the Elim Evangelical Church in Bedford Street.

At 8.50 am, four HE bombs fell in Southwick, three around the Village Green the other in Wellington Street. At 41 The Green, owned by Luxdon Laundry, a direct hit, caused extensive damage. Trapped in the wreckage were pensioners Mary Elizabeth Taylor (66), and Adam Fairley (66), and on being extricated from the shattered building both were found to be quite badly hurt.

William Otterson (58) was slightly hurt and a WAAF, who happened to be passing, joined the rescue efforts and helped to comfort some children who were brought from an adjoining building suffering from shock.

A second bomb fell outside 45 The Green, ripping up 30 feet of pavement, a gas main which caught fire and electricity cables. At first, owing to the darkness, it was not possible to deduce if this bomb had exploded and it was treated as a uxb and 16 people were evacuated.

Another bomb demolished a disused workshop, at the rear of The Green, which was in the process of being pulled down. This bomb apparently fell between 2 public shelters which were in use, but were undamaged.

The fourth bomb fell immediately next to the end wall of 1 Wellington Street. Occupying the ground floor were Henry and Catherine Fitzsimmons and their nine children who were fortunately sheltering in the pub cellar opposite. Mr Fitzsimmons standing in the doorway had to dive inside for cover.

Upstairs were bricklayer George and Ada Lynn and their children Robert (20), Agnes (18), Ethel (15), Margaret (11), George (8) and 2-year-old Kenneth. All were sitting in the kitchen when the bomb exploded and the whole house fell around them. None of them were hurt, but their exit to the street was blocked. Locals from a pub opposite rushed to their aid and managed to quickly rescue them. A neighbour later told the *Sunderland Echo*: 'It was a miracle that they survived. They were just like chimney sweeps when we got them out.'

One of these bombs fell 50 yards from The Savoy cinema but most of the audience remained in their seats.

On the south side of the river, at 21 Stockton Road, an unexploded anti-aircraft shell came back to earth into the backyard, partially demolishing a dividing wall. A small number of residents were evacuated while this was dealt with. The nose cap of another shell fell through the roof of 23 Rothsay Street.

41 The Green, Southwick, where two people had to be rescued from the debris.

Some of the children who were rescued from 1 Wellington Street. Ethel (15), Margaret (11) George (8) and Kenneth (2) Lynn.

Rear of The Green, Southwick.

After dropping its bombs, and machine gunning parts of Sunderland, the aircraft cut its motors and glided out of the searchlight zone and headed east out to sea.

Between 3.40 am and 4.00 am, Friday the 11th, heavy anti-aircraft fire was heard over the town, but there was no damage reported.

So ended Sunderland's first full year of war. Although bombed on a number of occasions, the town had, as yet, not suffered the same kind of wholesale destruction and loss of life as London or Coventry. The nation's capital was in the middle of its 'blitz' when the Luftwaffe called every night for months on end. Casualties at Coventry from the night of 14th November 1940 totalled many more than Sunderland suffered during the whole war.

A Messerschmitt 109 fighter that had been shot down in Kent during the Battle of Britain, toured the country to raise money for War Weapons Week, which in Sunderland was during November 1940.

Under armed guard, the Messerschmitt on display at Turvey's Garage in Holmeside.

FAMOUS LANDMARKS
BLITZED
1941

The Winter Gardens in Mowbray Park badly damaged in the raid of 15/16th April 1941.

The weekend beginning Friday, 21st February 1941 saw Wearside gripped by severe winter weather, the worst in living memory. Power lines had been brought down due to the weight of snow and ice. This caused the deaths of two youngsters, one treading on a power line and his friend as he tried to pull him clear. During Saturday all trams and buses in Sunderland were withdrawn for 24 hours. At the time little was reported in the press due to censorship, but at one point it was feared that Sunderland would be cut off.

On Sunday, the 23rd, another bitterly cold night, the sound of an aircraft was heard flying over the town at around 8.40 pm. Four minutes later the sirens were sounded, followed 3 minutes later by the sound of explosions. Four bombs had fallen, in Tunstall Vale, Ennerdale and Cairo Street.

Arriving in Tunstall Vale at 9.00 pm, PC William Fawcett together with Sergeant James Byrne and PC Alec Greenlay found a scene of confusion. After a quick look around, the policemen found that several houses had been demolished and many others badly damaged. People were trapped at Nos 3, 20 and 22. All the phones in the street had been rendered inoperable, so the officers set up their incident post in nearby Brookside Terrace. Once there, a warden brought incident lamps and set them down in a pile of snow at the front door. From here, the policemen set about organising the rescue efforts.

At No 3, a fruit shop, 5 people were trapped, including a baby. PCs Natrass, John Doyle and an army officer together with the Reverend Haswell from Christ Church tried to reach those trapped through a passage, but they found their way was blocked. Other policemen, including a Superintendent Smith, residents and wardens set up a chain in the passage to pass out debris.

First to be recovered, after about half an hour, was shop owner Alfred Sharp (65). At this point a Dr Cramb arrived and quickly examined Mr Sharp and said he was in no danger and to release him. As this was going on the all clear sounded at 9.54pm. Ten minutes later Sharp was brought into the passage and his injuries were treated. He was later taken to the Royal Infirmary.

Five minutes later Mr Sharp's eldest daughter, Mrs Violett Cowell (29), was brought out from the wreckage and carried into the passage where Dr Cramb pronounced her dead.

By this time Doyle and Natrass were under the wreckage of the kitchen when they discovered a fire. Calling for a stirrup pump and volunteers from nearby houses to carry buckets of water to assist in extinguishing the fire. All this time the police and volunteers had to use their bare hands and borrowed tools to assist in clearing debris as the ARP services had not yet arrived. In fact, Superintendent Edward Smith, the Deputy Chief Constable had constables enquire about the delay of the rescue services. This turned out to be due to

The Fruiteres at 3 Tunstall Vale. Baby David Cowell was found by rescuers in room marked by the arrow.

difficulty in starting vehicles due to the freezing conditions and many of the roads were impassable with snow.

Soon after Mrs Cowell's body was recovered, the 2 other trapped women were recovered from the debris, but both Irene Sharp (27) and Mrs Amelia Sharp (63) had been killed.

When Mr Sharp had been rescued he gave details of who was in the house at the time the bomb fell and he indicated that baby David Cowell was close to where he was located, next to his mother at the far side of the kitchen. On this information, the rescuers continued work to try to find baby David. All the debris behind the collapsed kitchen ceiling was removed by the policemen and 2 of the demolition squad, but the child was not found. Most people at the incident agreed

20 Tunstall Vale.

that if the child was in the debris his chances were hopeless.

It was then almost 1.00 am on the 24th, and most of the policemen had been taken off duty, PC Levick being left in charge at the ruins of the fruit shop, while the rescue squads continued their search through the night for the baby.

At his home in Belle Vue Drive, off duty policeman Sergeant Usher saw the flash of the bombs exploding. Making sure his wife and child were in their shelter, he made his way to Tunstall Vale. At No 7, he was informed that a woman, Isabella Dobing (61) was trapped by debris. Entering her house by the front door, he quickly found that he couldn't reach the woman. Going to the back of the house he scaled a wall and crawled through a hole and into the house. 'I called out, asking the woman where she was. Receiving a reply, I started to remove some bricks, plaster, slates and other material. After removing several bricks, I saw hair, and after clearing away further debris was able to remove most of the masonry from around her head and shoulders.' Sergeant Usher was by then being assisted by Phillip Kirkupp and Special Constable Patterson, however the space for rescue was extremely limited. Usher went on in his report: 'The woman showed great courage, and after warning me that she was not dressed, asked if I could release her legs. I made an endeavour to remove what appeared to be a table, but this was held in position by heavy woodwork.'

At this point the rescue services arrived to take over the work. Leaving No 7, Usher went to the junction of Tunstall Vale and Briery Vale to direct traffic and to stop unauthorised entry to Tunstall Vale. Many ambulances were having difficulty negotiating the road conditions, Usher and others giving a helping hand or shoulder to get them on their way.

Sgt Usher then saw the lady he had been trying to rescue on a stretcher, being taken to an ambulance. The stretcher tipped and the woman fell off into the snow, adding insult to her injuries. Sgt Usher then helped to get her safely to the ambulance, where she was taken to the Royal Infirmary. Mary Thompson (76) of 7 Tunstall Vale was killed.

Further up Tunstall Vale more people were trapped. At 9.10 pm PCs David Naylor, Crosbie and Metcalf found themselves at the rear of Tunstall Vale, at the demolished houses, Nos 20 and 22. After being told that a man, Jim Crow (32) was trapped in number 22, Naylor later reported: 'Climbing over the wreckage to the kitchen, we then searched the wreckage, and could hear a man's voice faintly beneath us.' After about 45 minutes they succeeded in releasing Mr Crow. His face was covered in mud and blood from a cut on his forehead.

After releasing Crow, the policemen learned that next door at No 20, a woman and child were trapped. There seemed to be great activity there and for a few minutes the constables, now joined by PC Alec Greenlay, did not go into the house in case they impeded any rescue work. However, on learning that a further three people were trapped they joined in the rescue attempt.

Naylor said: 'One of the women was trapped in an upright position and while giving her a drink I heard a voice requesting water and then discovered a man behind me completely buried. Greenlay and I at once went to his assistance. We worked for sometime and it became apparent that we could not possibly release him without causing debris to fall on the woman.' By now a large crowd had gathered, but to the rescuers' consternation only succeeded in getting in the way of the light of the few torches they possessed.

Those trapped included an elderly man, two women, a girl and a baby, all grouped together around the fire place, within about nine feet of each other. PC Greenlay saw: 'A woman trapped from the waist downward and lying alongside her, a baby with only its rear quarters showing out of the bricks and mortar, a large plank lying across its back. Nearby another woman was lying head downwards with only her legs showing.'

The man was trapped in a kneeling position by a heavy plank, bricks and mortar across the backs of his legs. A space was cleared around the man's head and he told his rescuers that he was uninjured.

Using only their hands, the policemen found digging and the removal of debris extremely difficult. PC Crosbie, a Special Constable and Sergeant Chapman eventually succeeded in releasing a woman, who was still alive, but seriously injured.

Lying his full length and practically buried, PC Greenlay managed, after some time, to reach the plank pinning the man amongst the rubble, and raised it sufficiently for the man to free his legs. The man was the last of those trapped at No 22 to be rescued. The policemen then dealt with a fire burning in the hearth with a stirrup pump.

Tragically Antoinette Sloan (21), her six-month-old daughter Joyce and Margaret Armstrong (23) were killed. A two-year-old named Armstrong was seriously injured as were John (46), Antoinette (45) and Winnie (11) West.

Others that night had narrow escapes and none more so than Mr and Mrs C.J. Walker and their daughter, who were neighbours of the Sharps. Returning home from church, they were only yards from their house when the bomb fell. Mr Walker told the *Sunderland Echo* the following day: 'We were walking down the street when my wife dropped her torch in the darkness and had to spend several minutes searching for it. We were about 25 yards from the front door when the bomb fell. If my wife had not dropped the torch we would have got in the house.'

*Right:
Grangetown
anti-aircraft
battery.*

*Left: ATS
receiving
instruction at
the anti-aircraft
battery at
Grangetown.*

*Right: Anti-
aircraft gunner
cleaning a
camouflaged
gun barrel at
Grangetown
battery, 1941.*

In a flat opposite the fruiterers, Mrs Holborn was dressing her son (12) and 10-year-old daughter to get them into their shelter in the yard, when the house rocked on its foundations: 'The ceiling and part of the roof fell in on us, knocking us to the ground. My daughter was buried in the debris, but I was soon able to get her out and she was not hurt apart from cuts and bruises.'

Many incendiary bombs were dropped, in the area bounded by the north-side of Villette Road, east by Corporation Road, south by Spelter Works Road and west by Ryhope Road, causing relatively little damage.

Harry Kay (41) of 19 Stratford Avenue, found an incendiary had set fire to his garden fence, but he quickly extinguished this with sand. Another incendiary fell in the street and he doused the bomb with water, which promptly exploded, injuring him in the throat.

PC Calyer was on his way to his air raid post when he saw fires on roofs in Percy Terrace. After returning home for his stirrup pump, he returned to the fires with neighbour Richard Wilkinson, to No 45 where they found an incendiary burning in the false attic, which they soon had under control. At No 50, incendiaries had fallen, one each, in front and rear bedrooms, and four had landed in the front and back garden of No 55.

In Hastings Street, No 95 had been badly damaged. The incendiary had entered the front dormer bedroom window, the blackout curtains immediately catching fire. The window frame was destroyed as were some articles in the room. The bomb went on to burn a hole in the floor and brought down much of the downstairs front room ceiling. Miss Maud Stanley was in the house at the time: 'I heard the plane and then the thud of bombs. I looked out of the window and saw flames. It was then that I heard a terrific crash and said to father, "Dad, we've got it." We went into the front room and heard crackling upstairs. Father rushed upstairs with sandbags and I went next door for Mr Nixon the warden.'

PC Armstrong was at home at 157 Cairo Street when the sirens sounded. Seconds later he heard something fall at the front and rear of the house. Looking out of his back door he saw two incendiaries burning themselves out in about 3 foot of snow. The same happened to the one at the front of the house.

Armstrong then saw a fire burning in the house next door. The bomb had fallen through the roof and was burning on the bedroom floor. Together with neighbours, Armstrong extinguished the blaze with a stirrup pump and sand while the occupiers, the Maddisons, were oblivious to the drama in their house as they were in their shelter.

In another street, incendiary bombs fell on a cottage, piercing the roof and setting fire to bedding. A member of an AFS party saw the bomb fall and ran towards the house, but the concussion of its fall threw him on his back. Recovering, the fireman and his colleagues got the fire under control by throwing the blazing bedding into the street.

Mr L.B. Crosby heard a bomb fall on his roof and climbed out of a bedroom window and onto the roof to tackle the fire.

A total of 41 fires were reported that night.

As some normality returned to the various incidents, a rescue party was still searching the ruins of 3 Tunstall Vale for baby David Cowell. For more than 10 hours the men toiled and all hope of finding the child alive was fading when soon after daybreak a faint cry was heard coming from the remains of an upstairs bedroom. The rescuers quickly moved to the rear bedroom where most of the roof, ceiling and rear wall had been blasted away and there, lying in his cot they found baby David. His life had been miraculously spared, as a bed next to his cot was covered in rubble. Part of the ceiling had fallen into the cot, but had missed David. He was rushed to the Royal Infirmary where he was treated for exposure.

Around 30 people were made homeless, but most had found alternative accommodation by morning.

A week after the bombing, on the 28th February, in a letter to the ARP Controller, McIntire, Dr Hebblethwaite quoted an extract from a report of the Tunstall Vale incident made by Mr Gregson, a casualty services officer: 'It seems pretty evident that far too many people assume the position of Officer in Charge irrespective of which organisation they belong to. This was, to my mind a serious matter. Numbers of people seemed ever ready to look on and give advice; others were countermanding the orders given by myself for the removal of casualties. As this is a matter in which I feel competent in doing myself, I do not welcome the presence of such people no matter how good their intentions have been.'

'I instructed the first aid party that the patient Mr Sharp should be removed to hospital at once. This was also the advice of Dr Cramb who was also on the scene of the incident.

The first aid party leader reported to me that the ambulance was being retained for further casualties whereupon I had to leave my job and see the instructions were carried out.'

A few nights later on Monday 3rd March, German aircraft, based mainly in Northern France and Holland, were over the north-east. The installations around the Tyne Estuary and Newcastle were the main targets, bombs falling between 8.08 pm to 9.05 pm.

In Sunderland, the sound of aircraft had been heard overhead for some minutes previous to the sirens sounding at 9.01 pm and soon afterwards a number of incendiary bombs were dropped in a area east of Hendon Dock and south of Lawrence Street, next to South Dock. More incendiaries and a HE bomb fell in South Dock.

ARP personnel with the cot.

Winston Churchill and Sir Arthur Lambert, during the Prime Minister's visit to the region in February 1941.

Damage from the high explosive bomb was considerable, as it exploded close to the switch gear house, almost demolishing the building. The switch gear which was used to raise and lower sheer legs, which were also damaged. Timber merchants Joseph Thompson had an engine house and a small office demolished, and a timber-built building, had a side 40 yards long blown out. Panes of glass in the dock master's house were shattered, the roof of an air compressor house was blown off and an electric crane belonging to the River Wear Commissioners was damaged. The 9,000-ton steamship *Empire Surf* lying alongside the dock quay had 14 plates and a cabin door damaged.

Sergeant James Byrne, with 2 constables, saw a huge glow in the sky in the direction of South Dock and on investigation found a raging fire at J. Thompson's dock office under the sheer legs, and incendiary bombs burning at G. Horsley's timber yard. All the fires were extinguished within half an hour.

At 28 Wall Street, lived 58-year-old Grace Bowman, an invalid lady. She was sitting in her living room with her sister-in-law Mrs Elizabeth Hazard (42), of Cousin Street, when an incendiary bomb crashed through the roof and into the living room. It burst into flames and set fire to Mrs Bowman's clothing. Because of her disability she was in some difficulty. Mrs Hazard was knocked heavily against an iron fireplace, so heavily that it was thought she had fractured her skull.

Street fire-watcher Francis Carr (17), who lived opposite Mrs Bowman, was running down Wall Street to tackle one of the other incendiaries when he heard cries for help. Mr Carr, told the *Sunderland Echo* the following day: 'Knowing she was an invalid, I immediately opened the door and went inside. I was driven back by dense fumes. I put my muffler round my mouth and entered the sitting room. It was impossible to see a thing but I groped around in the dark until I came across Mrs Bowman lying across a chair by the fireside. Her clothing was smouldering, and I dragged her out into the street.

She was conscious and kept saying: "She's in there, she's in there." Gathering that another woman was in the house I went back. After groping around again I found Mrs Hazard lying unconscious in the fireplace. I dragged her out and had just got her on the pavement when I heard a high explosive bomb whistling down.' Carr then shielded the injured women from any blast, but fortunately the bomb fell far enough away from them to hurt them. PC Emlyn James and a lady warden arrived and gave first aid to the women, who were then taken to the Royal Infirmary. PC Natrass and local residents extinguished the fire. As Mr Carr walked from the incident, he collapsed due to his efforts and the effects of smoke, however he had recovered enough to be able to go to work as usual at 5.30 am as a newspaper dispatcher.

Francis Carr, who rescued two women from a blazing house.

Also in Wall Street, at least 2 incendiaries fell through the roof of the house belonging to Mr J.G. Swainston, a train driver. Mr Swainston was at work at the time, while his wife was at a neighbour's across the road. On seeing the fires she rushed to the house where the fires were in the false attic, living room and scullery. George Downs helped Mrs Swainston by squeezing himself into the attic, which by now was well ablaze, but he managed to extinguish the fire with stirrup pump and sand. One of the bombs fell through the roof, drilled a hole in a frying pan, smashing the top of the cooker, setting fire to some sand bags placed in the kitchen for fire-fighting purposes. Mrs Swainston was pictured in the *Sunderland Echo* the following day holding the holed frying pan.

Mrs Swainston, with her frying pan holed by an incendiary bomb.

A number of men using stirrup pumps tackled incendiaries at 41 Wear Street, where John Wilson (26), sustained injury to his left hand. Two families lived at No 41. John Haynes, his wife and 2 children aged 7 and 11 occupied the upstairs, while downstairs were Mr Ed Watson, his wife and 4-year-old and 9-year-old children, all of whom were unhurt. Damage was caused to the roof and ceiling at the front of the house, destroying a sofa, wardrobe and all the Hayes' clothing.

Two further incendiaries fell in the yard at 38 Wear Street and in the roadway of Lawrence Street near to the Ash Bar public house. These were quickly covered with sand and caused no damage.

Soon after the first bombs fell, six HE bombs fell in a direct line between Rectory Park School, Paley Street and the water tower of Sunderland Corporation Electricity Company, in Farringdon Row, one falling only 100 yards from the tower.

Potentially the most serious of these bombs fell on the rear of the Bill Quay or Gill Cemetery air raid shelter, where Sergeant J. Cooke was on duty. Cooke found that the explosion had damaged the shelter roof and caused part of the walls to collapse. Because of the damage, lights were showing through the roof, Cooke saw to it that the bulbs were removed in case the glow attracted further bombing. Fortunately the rear or second section of the shelter was seldom used and was unoccupied. Those people in the first section were uninjured.

Craters were found in Back Hopper Street, on ground that had been cleared under the slum clearance scheme, near to the cemetery boundary wall and in Ayre's Quay Road.

In Rectory Park School, a bomb fell in the yard, but caused little damage to the school buildings, no doubt unhappily for the children.

The next raid had the sirens sounding at 8.20 pm Friday, 14th March and 25 minutes later a number of bombs fell on the north side of the river, all the bombs falling amongst residential property. The all clear sounded at 2.22 am.

The worst incident was in Francis Street, Roker, where a large bomb demolished Nos 43, 44, 45, and 46 and seriously damaged many more houses. Debris was thrown up on to Redby School and damaged ambulances parked there. At No 44 a number of people were trapped and rescuers were being hampered by escaping gas.

Members of the fire service arrived within 3 minutes of the bomb dropping. Commencing a search they heard a faint cry from under their feet, Fireman Hawick, Auxiliary Firemen Morse, Swanston and Wyness began clearing away the rubble with their hands and after about 10 minutes Mr Lewis Viner (72) was uncovered followed soon after by Mrs Viner and one of their daughters. Both women were unconscious, but breathing, but there was no sign of life from Mr Viner.

To get to those trapped, the firemen had to remove parts of the roof and bricks from the kitchen area of the house. While some held up other parts of the collapsed roof. Two firemen went underneath to remove more rubble. Gas pipes were located and sealed. On moving a beam and some furniture the men found 35-year-old Nora Viner who was quickly rescued, placed on a stretcher and tended to by a member of the St John Ambulance Brigade. Mrs Emma Viner (74), and daughter Emma (39) were both seriously injured.

At No 46, Fire Sergeant Douglas was told that 2 women were trapped. Firemen were already digging in what was the centre of the house. Douglas climbed into a hole the firemen had made and found the heads of the women protruding from the wreckage. Mrs Sarah Alice Pennell (50) and her daughter Marie (18), were found clasped in each other's arms. Within 15 minutes both had been released, but both were dead. Joseph Pennell was rescued with slight injuries.

Another bomb fell in Duke Street North, demolishing Nos 31, 32 and 33. Again people were trapped but, on being rescued were found to be only slightly injured.

In Roxburgh Street, another bomb demolished a house, and damaged several others.

At No 46, the Atkinson family were trapped. Rescued slightly hurt were Ada Atkinson (26), three-year-old Stanley and Mary (18) while 71-year-old retired tobacconist George Atkinson was uninjured, but 55-year-old Mary Elizabeth was killed. Hours later budgies were heard talking from amongst the wreckage. Although the Atkinson's had a shelter in their yard they were not using it during this raid. The shelter was totally destroyed.

Recalling the incident almost exactly 53 years later from his home in Berkshire, Richard Watson wrote: 'When the air raid

All that remained of Nos 30, 31 and 32 Duke Street North, Roker, after a direct hit.

siren sounded mother, sister and myself and the dog went as usual to the brick shelter in the back yard of No 38 Roxburgh Street – my father worked for LNER, was at Blyth as a crane operator (only returning home at weekends). The usual recommended equipment was already on site - blankets, paraffin lamp, candles, stirrup pump and gas masks. The civilian type respirators had in fact been assembled by us at the beginning of the war at the All Saints Church parish hall in Fulwell Road where my mother was a caretaker. It was used as a centre to both assemble and issue them. It is surprising after so long afterwards I can still sense that smell of new rubber and recall the scene with

46 Roxburgh Street, Roker.

the piles of boxes and folding tables on which the volunteers were doing their work.

A couple of hours after the warning I left the shelter and went into the house to make some tea and refill a thermos. The sky was lit up with searchlights and exploding flak – we had heard the bombers and their loads being dropped and it seemed we were in for another long night. The door from the garden and the yard opened into the kitchen but when I went in I turned right into the living room for some reason. We had adequate blackout curtains so I put on the light and went toward the fireplace. The next thing that happened was an almighty bang, the house shook, the lights went out and the walls appeared to collapse inwardly with bricks and soot falling down the chimney into the fireplace. I had a torch in my pocket and with this saw it was clear that there was no way out of the house through the door. Rubble had piled up blocking the exit completely. My first thought was for the family – had the shelter been hit? I pulled down the blackout curtains which were still in place. We had the standard strips of paper stuck to the glass and they had served their purpose as the window was broken but had stayed in one piece. Not for long however. The only obvious exit – a couple of swift bashes with a chair and I got out into the yard. The shelter was still there. A few bricks had dropped onto it but that was of no consequence, My mother, sister and dog 'Chips' were taken to either Redby School or the Parish Hall which were emergency centres prepared for such incidents. I went to see what help I could give to the rescue services.

We were several houses away from the impact point of the bomb (No 46). The official report however of "slightly damaging" other houses surprises me. As a result of the damage our family had to go to relatives in Benwell, Newcastle for several months, until repairs were completed. Indeed we were there when I started my apprenticeship at Vickers Armstrong in June 1941.

At the time of the bombing I was holding a temporary job as a very junior assistant at Piper's, the "high class grocers" in town. Mr Piper used to stand by the door at 8.30 am when the staff arrived rebuking those who were late even by a minute. Having been helping out at the bombed area most of what was left of the night I had got only an hour or so's sleep and went to work at about 9.30 am. The shop was full of the "high class" customers by then. Mr Piper came from behind the counter clearly extremely displeased with me and very angry. "Mr Watson, Mr Watson," he called very loudly (I was only 15), "Do you realise you are LATE, very LATE. There can be no POSSIBLE excuse!" I really lost my temper. "Mr Piper" I said, just as loud as he: "I've been bombed out of my home and all night I've been helping get people out of what was left of theirs. And you are concerned that I'm not here to cut up your bacon. Goodbye!" I probably worded it a bit stronger than that. I then walked out.'

A 250kg uxb was found at 13 Inverness Street, Roker, and a number of houses were evacuated.

Another bomb fell in Sandringham Road, Roker. People close to where the bomb fell suffered slight injuries, including warden Austin Trewhitt, who was attached to 3B Post in Roker Baths Road. Trewhitt (31) of Westburn Terrace, accompanied by some fire-fighters were making their way towards the Roker Park football ground when they heard the whistle of falling bombs close by and dropped to the ground to get what cover they could in Leeds Street. As the bombs exploded, Trewhitt was hit by debris and found himself under a gable end wall which was close to collapsing. Warden Thomas Binding, a neighbour of Trewhitt's, then collapsed from his injuries and Trewhitt and Fire-watcher Lawther assisted Binding to a house in Sandringham Terrace, where Trewhitt also collapsed. Trewhitt was taken to the Monkwearmouth and Southwick Hospital while Binding had his wounds treated at Colliery Schools first aid post at the Wheatsheaf. Also injured at this time was Harry Meldrum (25), of 17 Westburn Terrace, who had been struck by splinters around the head.

The gable end that Trewhitt had found himself under was the bedroom of 70-year-old James Newton, who was asleep. Mr Newton's son, who was deaf, was sleeping downstairs when he felt the shock waves of the exploding bomb.

Going to his father's assistance, he found him covered with debris, still on his bed. Newton's daughter thought her father was dead, but he soon recovered, but bemoaned the fact that the incident had made him late for his work as an engine fitter.

Others living nearby included George Morris, his wife and eight-year-old son, who were in a brick shelter when a bomb fell between them and the house. The house was completely demolished, but the shelter, only completed days before, didn't have a brick displaced.

Next door to the Morris family lived joiner Robert Spicer (65), his wife and daughter Brenda (22). Hearing the bomb falling, the Spicer's dashed for a cupboard. Mr Spicer recalled for the *Sunderland Echo*: 'Before I had time to get up from my chair I was knocked down by blast and debris and fastened against the cupboard door. I was unable to talk, but I could hear them shouting that they were alright and calling my name.'

Rescuers managed to free the Spicers from the wreckage within fifteen minutes, Mr Spicer having lacerations all over his body, his wife and daughter being unhurt.

Another neighbour, George Eames (50), had no shelter of his own and saw his wife off to a friend's shelter. Planning to go to bed, Mr Eames decided to call in on his wife as she was very nervous during the raids. Mr Eames had just got to the friend's house when the bomb demolished his own.

The roof and stands at Roker Park were holed and it was reported that there were 6 uxb's on the pitch.

By comparison, the next incursion of Sunderland's airspace by the Luftwaffe, during the night of Monday 7th and Tuesday 8th April, was insignificant. Warning 'Red' was received at 9.03 pm. The drone of aircraft and anti-aircraft fire were heard intermittently over the town.

Half-an-hour after midnight, a small HE bomb fell on the footpath at the

Repairs being made to the roadway in Cleveland Road, caused by a single HE bomb.

junction of Cleveland Road and General Graham Street, making a small crater, damaging a gas main. Nos 34 and 36 Cleveland Road received slight damage. The Gaiety Theatre in High Street East was damaged by part of an anti-aircraft shell falling back to earth. No-one was hurt at either incident.

The all-clear sounded at 3.12 am. The sirens sounded again at 3.41 am, the all-clear at 4.48 am.

Raids during April, saw the demise of some of Sunderland's more noted buildings.

The alert sounded at 11.25 pm, Wednesday, 9th April, but it wasn't until 1.45 am on Thursday that the first bombs crashed to earth. A large number of incendiary bombs fell in the centre of town, between Crowtree Road, Frederick Street, High Street and Borough Road. Other incendiaries fell close to Hendon Paper Works in Commercial Road and in Dykelands Road, Fulwell.

Some of the bombs fell on to the roof of the Binns Store on the west side of Fawcett Street and the top floor in the centre of the building was soon blazing. Although the regular and Auxillary Fire Service were in action very quickly, flames soon spread throughout the store. It seems that initially only 2 appliances were requested, but as reports came into the incident post at the Gas Office, Fawcett Street, a request for all possible fire engines were to be sent to Fawcett Street, only 25 minutes after the bombs had started falling, an indication of just how rapidly the fire spread.

Close to Binns was Police Inspector Rouse, who saw that part of the Town Hall roof was on fire. Entering through the side door, Rouse climbed the stairs of the tower into the attic and when assistance arrived, tackled the blaze with stirrup pumps, in the process being very fortunate not to be seriously injured

Firemen damping down Binns Store. Note hoses along Fawcett Street bringing water from the river to help fight the fires.

Fawcett Street shrouded in smoke.

as his trousers were burnt by molten lead from the roof.

By this time fires were blazing at Steels, Wilkinson's Garage and the Northumbria Printing Works, all situated in Holmeside, and at Hector Grabham in Blandford Street.

Inspector Rouse then saw a fire taking hold near to the top of the Sunderland Gentlemen's Club. Again, making his way upstairs, in total darkness, passing an elderly woman on the way, he eventually found an incendiary alight in the attic above a bathroom. Trying to climb into the attic, Rouse lost his balance and fell into the bath which was full of water. Then looking to turn off the electric meter he received a shock but still managed to switch the meter off, then returned to putting out the fire.

Rouse then made his way to the roof of Binns foodstore, which in his report said there were no signs of fire on any building on the east side of Fawcett Street, but he did find the remains of two incendiaries burnt out on Binns roof, and one on the roof of the Health Department. Rouse could hear the sound of aircraft overhead. The time was about 3.30 am.

It is here that reports differ as to how the east side Binns Store was set on fire.

Some suggest that sparks and embers were the cause while Inspector Rouse believed at the time, and indeed wrote in his report, that further incendiaries were dropped. There is also the possibility that incendiaries had penetrated the roof and lay smouldering for some time, before bursting into flame. What is certain is that German bombers were over Sunderland at this point, as around 3.30 am HE bombs fell in Hudson Dock and Back Ethel Street, Hendon.

Whatever the cause, Binns Store on the east side of Fawcett Street was soon burning fiercely. The Deputy Chief Constable ordered the River Wear fire vessel, the *Fire Queen*, up river to a point close to Wearmouth Bridge to allow hoses to be connected to the ones in use in Fawcett Street.

At 4.30 am the telephone at the incident post at the Gas Office went dead, the post transferring to the railway offices at Burdon House.

Tackling a fire at the Juvenile Library in Fawcett Street, a policeman broke into the building and covered a bomb with a sand bag. The incendiary promptly exploded and the police and fire guards managed extinguish the fire with a stirrup pump.

At No 38 Holmeside, Rendcar & Gibbs, an incendiary bomb had exploded above a room used for dress-making. PCs McClelland and Thomas found the shop doorway open and made their way upstairs, but the pair were beaten back by dense smoke. Undaunted, they scaled a ladder and together with PC Plenderleith managed to put out the fire.

The burnt out shell of one of the Binns buildings.

Plenderleith, who had already put out burning incendiaries at the front door of the Conservative committee rooms using a door mat and sand, then went to the roof of Barnes, Welch & Barnes in Athenaeum Street to extinguish a bomb burning there, plus 2 more in the road in Holmeside. He then took a hose at Steels remaining there until that fire was under control.

The managing director of Hector Grabham, painters and decorators, of Holmeside, had been informed that the building had been hit by incendiaries. On entering the building, Mr Grabham found that a bomb had gone through the roof and second floor of the warehouse, coming to rest on the third step of a stairway and was: 'burning furiously' and was threatening to set alight to stocks of paint and turpentine. Helped by two members of the Blandford Street fire fighting section, this fire was quickly dealt with. In the yard, another incendiary had set the waste paper cupboard alight, which had spread to a staircase from the shop to the warehouse, and flames were getting through to the shop. Again, this was promptly extinguished. The Blandford Street fire fighters had dealt with 15 small fires within half an hour.

At about 3.35 am Sergeant Rutter with other constables saw a fire burning on the south side of Blackett's store in High Street West. It took the policemen some time to gain access to the building and when they did they were unable to get to the fire until a director of the firm had arrived. Using two stirrup pumps the men tackled the fire, which by this time had gained a considerable hold, and Rutter sent a request for AFS assistance. Soon after the policemen had to leave the building because of dense smoke.

At 4.20 am, the incident post informed Dr Stuart Hebblethwaite, medical officer in charge of casualty services, that his office at 27 Fawcett Street was in immediate danger from fire.

At 5.00 am, the caretaker at the town museum, reported an unexploded incendiary bomb in the Winter Gardens, which was removed by Sergeant Hill, and taken to the incident post. A number of incendiaries had fallen on to the roof of the museum. One crashing through the roof on to an exhibition of embroidery, but this was quickly dealt with by the caretaker's daughter using a sandbag.

Three further bombs lodged in the false roof of the museum gallery and fire guards experienced considerable difficulty in gaining access to extinguish them. Mowbray Park Terrace, outside the Winter Gardens was strewn with incendiaries and police and firemen shovelled them into the lake. Special Constable John Taylor was burned on the hand when one of the bombs burst.

As stated earlier, at around 3.30 am the sound of aircraft could be heard over the town. At this time, HE bombs fell at Hudson Dock and a large calibre bomb dropped in a yard in back Ethel Street, Hendon, close to the Londonderry railway sidings and a large set of signals. The explosion demolished 7 houses and damaged to varying degrees, a further 16. A number of people were trapped in the rubble of their homes, at Nos 10, 11 and 12 Ethel Street, and claimed the lives of John Bowe (17) of No 10 and Miss Laura Sinclair (24), of No 11 and seriously injured 9 people. Gas water and electric supplies were disrupted and 58 people were rendered homeless and were temporarily accommodated at Hudson Road School.

As daylight came, Wearsiders on their way to work were greeted with the sight of the still-smouldering burnt out shells of the Binns Stores shrouded in smoke and yards of hose pipes snaking across the street and firemen still damping down the fires. While hundreds came to gaze at the destruction, this raid demonstrated the destructive potential of the incendiary bomb.

Not only Wearside was bombed this night, as the Luftwaffe also targeted Tyneside. In South Shields many fires were started and the Shields fire service called on their Sunderland colleagues for assistance. Units that responded worked, for the most part, while bombs burst around them. Sunderland fireman Ralph Thorburn was killed on duty in South Shields. Rescue and demolition squads were also sent and were later commended for their work by the South Shields War Executive Committee.

Ethel Street, where two people were killed.

Six people were killed at 23 & 25 St Luke's Road, Pallion.

The night of 15th/16th April saw the Luftwaffe turn its might on Belfast, and as on previous raids to that city and others to the Clydeside area, Sunderland lay on the flight path of the bombers. However, it appears that other units made an independent attack on Wearside and Tyneside with 38 aircraft.

In Sunderland, the sirens sounded at 10.45 pm, which was soon followed by the sound of aircraft and intermittent gunfire.

At 2.20 am, the 16th, three HE bombs fell in Pallion, all within 100 yards. The first fell onto a house in St Luke's Road, demolishing Nos 23 and 25. A number of families lived there and were trapped in the wreckage.

From the few details recorded of this incident, it appears that 6 people were killed. The bodies of Margaret Henderson (25) and her 2-year-old daughter Doreen, were both recovered from the debris at around 7.00 am. An hour later, John Clarke (42), was found along with his daughters Rose (5) and Brenda (3). Francis South, of No 23½ was almost unrecognisable when recovered. Seventeen others were injured.

The other 2 bombs fell in the Sunderland Forge and Engineering Co, one in the testing room causing material damage and slightly affecting production, the other falling into an open yard. Five men, John Boddy (37), Ernest Harrison (35), Francis Home (53) George Nottingham (46) and warden William Saint (44) were killed at the works.

At 2.15 am, a shower of incendiary bombs fell 100 yards north of Chester Road, Grindon, close to a military camp, causing fires that were dealt with by the fire service. There were four bombs that had not exploded and those, together with other material from aircraft, were later taken to police headquarters.

It was at 3.50 am that a horrific weapon made its unwelcome introduction in Sunderland, The parachute mine. Designed to sink shipping, the mine was adapted for use against land targets. A conventional bomb normally exploded after it had penetrated the earth, and so much of the blast was absorbed,

The remains of the Victoria Hall, looking up Toward Road.

whereas the mine, suspended under a parachute, descending slowly, exploded on contact with the ground, the force of the blast being greater resulting in more damage.

That first mine did so much damage to 2 of the town's more famous buildings that they later had to be demolished – Victoria Hall and the Winter Gardens. The mine fell in Laura Street, next to the Victoria Hall, where on the 16th June 1883, 183 children were killed, crushed in a narrow passage.

After the ferocious blast of the mine, only the south wall and a few roof beams remained standing. Sergeant Hill and PC Berg were standing at the entrance of the trench air raid shelter in Burdon Road when the mine exploded hurling them both to the back of the shelter. The pair quickly recovered and ran down Burdon Road and Borough Road, shouting to the occupants of the Water Company Office in John Street and Palatine Hotel to extinguish their lights as windows and blackouts had been smashed. The 2 policemen then came across Miss Hilda Newton (28) who worked at the Palatine Hotel, in a car with severe head injuries. They took her to the nearest police-box and from there she was taken to the Royal Infirmary.

In Laura Street, 6 shops and the Oddfellows Hall had been demolished, the wreckage of the Oddfellows Hall was also on fire. Sgt Hill knew the caretakers at the Oddfellows Hall, Mr and Mrs Hazard, who lived on the upper floor. Together with another policeman, Sgt Hill then: 'Searched about where I knew the entrance to be when a voice said, "I'm here," and on entering a cavity found a man buried in debris up to the neck with both legs and left arm imprisoned and his right arm fast from the elbow to the shoulder.'

Joined by another policeman, the men removed rubble and pulled John Dobson clear. In doing this the men found the arm of another man protruding from wreckage, the head and body covered by wood and bricks. As the men began to clear this more debris fell due to a rescue party working above them. They tested the man for signs of life. Thomas Hazard (38), was found to be dead.

Missing in Laura Street were fire guard Stanley Foster (33) and an unnamed girl, but thought to be buried in the ruins of the Oddfellows Hall. Enquiries had been made at Foster's home, as he had been 'seen on the corner of Tavistock Place just moments before the mine exploded, but at 7.15 am it was reported to Thornholme that his body had been found in Laura Street.

There were numerous injuries sustained by people in the surrounding area and casualties were taken to the basement of Tatham Street Methodist Chapel to await the arrival of ambulances. Damage was caused to buildings as far away as Union Street.

A second mine fell in Back Hedworth Terrace, at the rear of Smyrna House in Symrna Place, a little further east of the first mine. One of the first on the scene was Inspector Sneddon. Sneddon and other policemen found that houses had been demolished in Hedworth Terrace and South Durham Street. Sneddon reported: 'On going over the debris I heard a mournful sound coming from a demolished house, 60 South Durham Street, where 2 families had been living.'

The police and rescue party set about extricating Mr Joseph Stephenson (78) who was taken to hospital but died on the 19th. Soon afterwards Mrs Isabella Stephenson (76) was found, but had been killed. The party continued to clear debris and next came across Henry Chapman (52), who was taken to the Royal Infirmary seriously injured. The rescuers had to saw through wood to remove debris from Mrs Jane Chapman (50), but she too was found to be dead. The c/o of the East Yorkshire Regiment made an officer and 15 men available to the rescue services at this incident.

As with Laura Street, damage to property was widespread and indeed it was a miracle that more people weren't killed. At least 10 people were injured. By 10.00 am, 280 people had reported to the Hudson Road School sleeping centre, due to their homes being uninhabitable.

Another mine landed on the beach, immediately south of the South Pier, but still managed to cause considerable damage. The huts belonging to the crew of the pier anti-aircraft gun were demolished. The roof and all the windows in Greenwell's ship repair yard damaged as was the lifeboat house.

South Durham Street, blasted by a parachute mine.

Property as far away as Roker Avenue on the north side of the river sustained damage, mainly broken windows.

At 3.57 am a report of parachutists seen in the vicinity of Tunstall Hills had been given to the police from Thornholme. Police and a detachment of the East Yorkshire Regiment were dispatched to make a search of the area, but nothing was found.

As for the Victoria Hall and the world-

Scrap metal collection, held early in 1941.

renowned Winter Gardens, both were shattered beyond repair and were later demolished.

It was noticed, 5 days later, that Edward William Bland (61) of 59 Back South Durham Street, had not drawn his pension, it was feared that he was still trapped in the wreckage of his shattered home. After enquiries by police to neighbours and family a search was made and at 5.45 pm his body was found. To the disgust of some policemen who had to guard Mr Bland's body, it was laid in the street for 2 hours while casualty service and transport service argued as to whose responsibility it was to collect Mr Bland. Eventually, and somewhat undignified, a lorry from the transport service collected Mr Bland.

During the night of Friday, 25th April, the Luftwaffe were again operating over the north-east, Sunderland docks being the principal target. In an attack that lasted from 9.55 pm to 11.10 pm, 57 aircraft dropped 80 tonnes of high explosives.

German radio claimed that explosions were claimed to have been observed in Hudson and Hendon Docks and at the north-west part of Thompson's

Unexploded bombs being cut up for scrap, March 1941. This photograph was not passed for publication by the censor at the time.

shipyard, starting numerous large and small fires. Apparently, the fires were seen over a great distance and were reported by an aircraft of the General Staff of the Luftwaffe engaged in an armed reconnaissance of the Firth of Forth. Despite these claims during Saturday morning, no bombs fell on Sunderland, all bombing taking place to Tyneside.

At 11.11 pm, Saturday, 3rd May, air raid warning 'Red' was received, but when the switch at police HQ to operate the sirens was activated, the sirens failed to sound. A message was transmitted to all warden's posts and the 'alert' was sounded by police and wardens using rattles and whistles. The all-clear sounded at 3.10 am, 4th May.

Shortly after midnight, a bomb fell in Stansfield Street School yard, causing considerable damage. A second bomb fell in Cromarty Street, a third in Duke Street North, a fourth in Osbourne Street, and a fifth in Brandling Street.

Outside Redby School, the caretaker's house in Cromarty Street and a cottage opposite were demolished. The occupants of the cottage escaped from their shelter unhurt. The school caretaker, Fred Garbutt and his wife, although not in their shelter, also escaped with slight injuries. They could count themselves fortunate. Normally during a raid, Mrs Garbutt took refuge under the stairs, but this night was lying awake in bed: 'My husband had just come into the house to see if I was all right when the bomb fell. I felt the bed going and pulled the bed clothes over my head to protect my face. When I felt the mattress come to rest on something solid, it was mixed up with debris several feet up from the ground. I pulled the bed clothes off my face. I could see daylight and smell gas faintly.'

Caught in the doorway, Fred was trapped by his feet. Rescue workers then arrived, Mrs Garbutt shouted to them: 'Don't worry about me, see to my husband.'

Fred was quickly released and Mrs Garbutt emerged from the wreckage, wrapped in a quilt and blankets, with injuries to her leg and bruising to her back. Indignant, she said: 'I had nearly finished my spring cleaning and Mr Garbutt had just finished painting the bathroom.'

Mrs Garbutt realised that it could have been more serious: 'If I had been under the stairs this time they would have been digging for me still and I probably would have been gassed.'

The occupants of 2 Duke Street North were Arthur Storey (45), his wife Edith and two daughters Audrey (4) and fourteen-month-old Edith Marion. They had left their home to join Frederick Foster (55), his wife Margaret (55) and her sister Mrs Louise Flett (60) (Edith Storey being their niece) in their brick surface shelter at 5 Duke Street North. At first it wasn't realised quite what had happened here. Three hours later, Sergeant Rutter reported 7 persons presumed trapped in 5 Duke Street North. After extensive inquiries regarding the whereabouts of those trapped, it was presumed that they were all killed when

The Redby School caretaker's house, in Cromarty Street, demolished in the early hours of 4th May 1941.

Duke Street North, was again badly hit.

their shelter received a direct hit by a bomb.

Probably the last person to see these people alive was warden John Nixon, who had left his post at Redby School around midnight to visit those in their shelters, calling in at No 5 at around 00.15 am.

Five days later, on 9th May, the grisly task of searching the wreckage was coming to an end when at 10.15 am, rescue service officer Ernest Antliffe, reported the recovery of remains of a body dressed in home guard uniform. It was Arthur Storey.

At 4 Westcott Terrace, the family of Mr and Mrs Turnbull, were in their shelter. Elsie (21) who had just registered for National Service that Saturday, Joan (19), James Campbell (12) and Maurice (8) were all fatally injured when a bomb exploded nearby. All were apparently still alive when rescued, but succumbed to their injuries by daybreak.

Living downstairs from the Turnbulls were William Wilson and his wife, who were in bed at the time of the explosion, but Mr Wilson managed to extricate himself and his wife from the wreckage, both suffering from shock.

Next door, at 5 Westcott Terrace, Mrs Margaret Moore (72) and her daughter Elizabeth (37), Mrs Mary Harvey (40) and her two-year-old daughter Anne and a neighbour Mrs Mary Usher (73) of number 7, were taking shelter under the stairs. Mr Robert Moore (70), a retired policeman, was on fire watching duty in a nearby street, when during a lull in the raid, made his way back home to see if his wife and daughter were safe. Mr Moore later told the *Sunderland Echo*: 'A few minutes previously, I had heard a bomb coming down not far away and with other men rushed around a corner and took what cover we could.' Picking himself up he continued on to his house: 'When I was approaching my home another bomb fell right in the street and I saw debris thrown into the air.' What Mr Moore had just witnessed was his own house receiving a direct hit: 'My wife and daughter were sheltering I knew, under the stairs. They would have had no chance at all.'

Also in their shelter at 10 Sandringham Road, were the Spanton family, when a bomb burst close by, killing Mrs Alice Jean Spanton (43), severely wounding her daughter Doris (19) and slightly injuring her husband Frank (41).

Around the same time, another bomb fell on the east side of Hendon Dock, about 30 feet from the quay. A second bomb fell at the south east corner of the same Dock and a third fell harmlessly into the sea. Two other bombs fell in the disused shipyard of Robert Thompson, known as Southwick Yard.

At 00.05 am incendiaries fell within an area of half a square mile from Corporation Road in the north to Henry Street to the south, from the Docks in the east to Hendon Road, causing several fires.

PC Maurice Fletcher was helping to extinguish fires at 7 Lilburn Street when he saw 4 Lawrence Street ablaze. The bomb had fallen through the roof at the rear of the house. Hurrying to the house with auxiliary fireman Plunkett, they found the house an inferno, and civilians attempting to tackle the blaze with stirrup pumps and buckets of water. Fletcher then advised those living at Nos 5 and 6 to evacuate their homes as flames were being blown in their direction. Soon after this the AFS arrived and quickly had the fire out, but not before the bathroom and kitchen were gutted and a bedroom seriously damaged. The persons living downstairs had already been bombed out on a previous occasion.

After smouldering for hours on a bed at 30 Wear Street, a fire started which was tackled by civilians and war reserve policeman W. Edge who managed to confine the damage to one room.

Around 70 people were evacuated from their homes in Stansfield Street, where it was believed that there was an exploded bomb, but on examination at first light it was found that it had exploded.

During the spring and early summer of 1941, German interests turned eastwards, to the Balkans and Russia. Many of the Luftwaffe bomber units were withdrawn from bases in western Europe to take part in these operations

Two men survey the damage caused in Brandling Street, Roker.

In an attempt to combat the effectiveness of the incendiary bomb, the government ordered that streets, shops and factories organise their own fire guards, such as these being given a demonstration in back Lonsdale Street, Roker in May 1941.

and there followed a lull in air attacks against Sunderland.

However, shipping in the North Sea continued to be targeted. Around 8 pm hours, Tuesday, 12th August, the SS *Eaglescliffe Hall*, 1,900 tons gross and with a crew of 24, sailed from Seaham Harbour, laden with coal. About an hour later she was attacked by an aircraft, a bomb exploding in the engine room. The chief engineer and a donkeyman were killed. The third engineer, a fireman, an able seaman, two Royal Artillery gunners and a naval gunner were wounded. The ship was later brought into the Wear and berthed at Corporation Quay. The injured were taken to the Royal Infirmary.

At 11.50 am the following day, many people saw a Heinkel 111 flying from the north-east, cross the coast and release bombs. The bombs fell into Mayswood Road, Fulwell, making 2 large craters, possibly being caused by 3 bombs, both craters being separated by only a few feet.

Tragically, the crater was where a semi-detatched house had stood, now totally demolished. At No 38, the body of Mr John Robson was recovered from the debris dead as were Mrs Isabella Easby (36) and her son Douglas William (4) from No 40. Two women in Mayswood Road were seriously injured and a woman and a 6-year-old boy from Prince George Avenue were slightly injured.

A busy River Wear during June 1941.

Property and money were found some distance from the scene and handed into the police.

Twenty houses were so seriously damaged as to be uninhabitable and houses up to 200 yards away were damaged. Gas, water and electricity supplies were effected. The sirens sounded minutes after the bombs had fallen and the alert was in force for almost an hour.

At 8.46 pm, Thursday, 11th September, acting Sergeant Blackburn was on duty in Hendon when he saw an enemy twin-engined aircraft. At a height of about 200 feet, with navigation lights showing, flying from the south, it was heading north in a line from Hendon Bridge to Gladstone Bridge in the South Docks.

The aircraft travelled about 100 yards north of Hendon Bridge when bombs were released, followed by two explosions, the second much more violent than the first. Both bombs fell in Hudson Dock.

On reaching Gladstone Bridge, the aircraft turned off its lights, turned towards the east and headed out to sea.

The bombs caused no damage or casualties. The industrial alarm was in operation at the time and the public alarm sounded immediately after the bombs had exploded.

Tuesday, 30th September, saw the Luftwaffe back over the town. The sirens sounded at 8.53 pm, the 'all-clear' at 11.00 pm. Two minutes before the alarm sounded, two bombs fell at the north-west outskirts of the Borough, one in a playing field, estimated at being at 500kg bomb, damaging nearby greenhouses. Another 500kg bomb fell in Reeds Field at Witherwack Farm. Ten minutes later, four more bombs, all thought to be 250kg, fell in Southwick, around three quarters of a mile from the first incident.

The worst incident occurred at 59 Shakespeare Street, the home of the Hackett family. Builders labourer William (44), his wife Gladys (42), Harry (16), Alice (10), and Thomas (5) were all killed as the house took the full force of the blast. It appears that the Hacketts had taken shelter under the stairs, and had not used their shelter for some time and thought the cupboard safer unless there was a direct hit. Mr Hackett had argued that the shelter was as likely to be hit as much as the house. On this occasion the shelter was undamaged. Twenty-year-old William George Hackett was initially named on casualty lists but had returned to his Royal Engineers unit at Doncaster.

At 68 Cato Street, the Hogan family were trapped and when eventually accounted for 19-year-old Nora and her 8-year-old brother Dennis had been killed, Mary (45) and Theresa (19) seriously injured and Denis (45), Mildred (12) and Terence slightly injured.

Bombs also fell in Cobham Square and in South Back Cobham Square. Nos 4, 5, 15 and 16 Cobham Square were badly damaged.

The final bomb fell at the north-west corner of Dryden Street. Here the Martin family owed their lives to the fact that they were in their Anderson shelter. Michael (46), Margaret, Theresa (13) and Ursula (10), were trapped in the shelter as rubble from their bomb blasted home blocked the exits. Mr Martin managed to remove part of the shelter rear wall and managed to extricate his family with the help of neighbours. Theresa told the *Sunderland Echo* the following day: 'I heard a loud noise which I thought was an aeroplane, but daddy knew it was a bomb coming down and told us to lie on the seats. The shelter jumped terribly and the seats gave way beneath us. My glasses and shawl were blown off by the blast.'

Another of Mr Martin's daughters, 18-year-old Margaret, took cover under an exterior staircase within sight of her home and saw: 'Her home go up in the air.' Margaret felt sure that her parents and sisters had been killed. Sixty-one people were rendered homeless, 22 of which were initially accommodated at the rest centre at West Southwick School. The police incident post complained of: 'a lack of co-operation between senior officers of all services.'

The Hackett family of Shakespeare Street, Southwick, were all but wiped out on the 30th September 1941.

Anderson shelter which saved the lives of the Martin family.

The night of Thursday, 2nd October, was one of anti-aircraft shelling. At 9.30 pm, it was reported that an anti-aircraft shell had fallen through the roof of a machine shop at British Ropes, in Fulwell, and had exploded. Damage to machinery resulted in a 5% to 10% loss in production and it was estimated that work wouldn't be fully restored for about a week.

Another shell exploded on the west side footpath, opposite 14 Fulwell Road, close to British Ropes. Two people were slightly hurt and 13 houses were slightly damaged. George Moffat (64) of 10 Fulwell Road was taken to Monkwearmouth and Southwick Hospital with an injury to his left index finger which had to be amputated, while Emmeline Smith (64) of 16 Fulwell Road was taken to Colliery School first aid post suffering from shock.

At 9.45 pm another shell fell through the roof of 6 Gloucester Avenue, Fulwell and exploded, blowing out the front window and extensively damaging the remainder of the house. An 81 year-old-lady was taken to hospital suffering from shock.

No bombs fell on the town, but for the ARP and public it must have been quite frustrating having to contend with not only German bombs but rogue anti-aircraft shells as well. More of these rogue shells caused damage to property during the night of Tuesday, 21st October. The siren sounded at 8.29 pm, the 'all clear' following at 10.35 pm.

At 8.50 am a shell fell onto 3 Riversdale Terrace, Durham Road, penetrating the roof and exploding on the upper floor of the three storey house, causing extensive damage. Four people were in the house at the time, although none was injured.

At the same time a HE bomb was heard to explode near to the junction of Newcastle Road and Shields Road, the device having fallen in a field between Southwick Quarry and Shields Road, owned by W. Reed of White House Farm.

The blast caused considerable damage to 9 Wells Gardens, situated 70 yards away which was owned by market gardener Stanley Stamp.

Ten minutes later another anti-aircraft shell fell in the front garden of 99 Ryhope Road, fracturing a gas main. As the shell failed to explode, nearby residents were advised to keep well away until the shell had been made safe. Another unexploded shell fell in Royden Avenue (off Ryhope Road).

The next raid on the town occurred on Friday, 7th November, during an alert of four-and-a-half hours. The siren sounded at 9.27 pm.

About 20 bombs fell on the town, the first of which was a pair heard to fall at the sea lock entrances to Hendon Dock, one at the south-east corner the other to the north-east corner. The first rendered inoperable the machinery that operated the Dock entrance bridge. The second bomb caused damage to the wall and entered the water.

At 10.24 pm, 4 bombs fell, the first in the precincts of the main electricity generating station in Farringdon Row. Damage was caused to numerous buildings, including a boiler house that was due to be demolished the following week. There was no interruption to electricity supplies. Another bomb fell on cottages in Lily Street. Four cottages were demolished and many others badly damaged.

At 8 Lily Street, retired policeman William Steel (74), was caught in the bomb blast and killed as he made his way to his shelter. His housemaid Margaret Holland (53), who was in the shelter, was hurt when the shelter collapsed. Next door, widows Mrs Pederson and Mrs Carter were unhurt, despite their shelter being on the edge of the crater. However, as the women crawled out of the shelter, Mrs Pederson was injured when she fell 12 feet into the crater.

Determined that the Luftwaffe would not disturb them from their chip supper were elderly couple James Robson and his wife, who were cooking when: 'the bomb came down and the house with it.' The couple, who were

The Electricity power station in Farringdon Row.

rescued after about 10 minutes, would normally have been in their shelter with their daughter and her three young children, but fortunately they had gone to a neighbour's shelter as theirs had a fused light. Their shelter was totally wrecked.

Another bomb fell on 11 Lambton Start of Lambton Drops, causing a large amount of damage. The other bomb fell in the Rock Top allotment gardens damaging cabins. About the same time another four bombs fell on the north side of the river Wear.

In Roker Avenue, a bomb made a direct hit on the Blue Bell public house, just 10 minutes after closing time. Only the manager, his wife Madeline Stephenson and a barmaid were still in the building. Joseph Cairns (26), was killed while standing outside the pub with two men when the bomb fell. The two men were injured and taken to hospital.

A bomb fell at the British Ropes Works in Portobello Lane, causing enough damage to interrupt production considerably. The third bomb fell directly opposite Tyzacks Brick Works in Fulwell Road, killing fire guard John Barrass (70).

The fourth bomb demolished 4 cottages in Fulwell Road. On his way home from a parade was Air Training Corps cadet Kenneth Humphries (17) when he heard the sound of an aircraft diving, as he walked along Fulwell Road. Hearing the whistle of bombs, he threw himself to the ground, followed by: 'a tremendous crash and bricks began to fall all around me.' Getting to his feet, Humphries couldn't see anything due to smoke and dust, but when this cleared he saw that a house had been demolished opposite from where he stood. This was 108 Fulwell Road. He later recalled: 'I could hear cries for help and ran across. There was a woman in the middle of the wreckage of one house pinned by a beam. I pulled the beam off her and got her out.' Nineteen-year-old Edna Gowland was taken to hospital with a suspected fracture to the base of her skull. Humphries had heard others crying out for assistance and the moans of those injured, so he ran to the police box outside the Cambridge Hotel, giving the officer on duty a precise location of the bombed houses, that greatly assisted in the quick release of those trapped. They included James

Gowland who was killed, his wife Ada and 16-year-old Eveline who were both seriously injured. Cadet Humphries' prompt and courageous actions are all the more praiseworthy when one considers that during his rescue efforts bombs were still falling.

Back on the south side of the river, at around 10.38 pm hours, a bomb fell in Whitehouse

One man was killed, and others injured standing outside the Blue Bell, Roker Avenue.

78

96-98 Fulwell Road, demolished in the raid of 7th November.

Road, Hendon, where a number of the Whitehouse Cottages were damaged. The bomb had exploded close to the LNER South Dock branch line.

At 1 Whitehouse Cottages, two women fire guards, Mrs. Madeline Elizabeth Smith (48), and Miss Madeline Smith (17), were killed as was 8-year-old Edwin Smith. 10-year-old William was seriously injured.

Whitehouse Cottages, Hendon

At 8 Whitehouse Road, Thomas Guest was standing in the doorway with Jimmy Sheraton, who lived upstairs, when a bomb fell nearby: 'Mother and my two sisters were with the Sheratons in the surface shelter.' Mr Guest then heard the sound of an aircraft diving followed by the whistle of bombs: 'I shouted duck, and Jimmy dived into the shelter. I had no time to do anything but fall flat before the house started coming down on top of me.' Mr Guest and the others escaped serious injury. After recovering he climbed over the rear wall of his yard, the door being blocked by debris and assisted ARP and other residents in rescue work being carried out at Whitehouse Cottages. Also killed at this incident was Joyce Armstrong (20). Three further bombs fell close to the railway embankment but all failed to detonate. About the same time more bombs fell in the region of South Dock. One fell on the docks railway line, hurling a steam train 20 yards down the track ending up overturned and at right angles to the track. The train was removed by 11.45 am, Saturday, the 8th, and the track reopened. The remaining bombs fell on the foreshore. Damage to property was reported in D'Arcy Street, Clementina Street and Ward Terrace close to the docks. Two hundred people were accommodated in rest centres immediately after the raid. Several roads were blocked but most were reopened by 6.00 am Saturday.

German radio broadcast, that harbour and industrial installations were attacked in a series of waves on Sunderland and that fires and explosions were observed.

At 10.11 pm, Monday, 8th December, when most Wearsiders were taking in the news of the Japanese attack at Pearl Harbour the previous day, the sirens sounded. At 10.55 pm bombs were heard exploding around Seaburn. This turned out to be 3 bombs falling on the foreshore about 70 yards from the promenade and 250 yards between each bomb. The blast blew out windows of the Seaburn Hotel, 6 shops, a concert hall and a number of houses on the promenade. Eight minutes later, 2 bombs fell in Cleghams Field, east of Queen Alexandra Road and north of Sea View Road, but caused no casualties or damage to property.

At 11.00 pm, 2 more bombs were heard to explode in the sea off South Dock. Twenty minutes later an anti-aircraft shell exploded on the road opposite 21 Westfield Grove, High Barnes, the shrapnel causing varying degrees of

Uxb recovery from fields to the south of the Eye Infirmary, which now forms part of the Southmoor School playing fields.

Right: ATS anti-aircraft gunners putting up Christmas decorations, December 1941.

Left: Cooks' inspection, Grangetown battery, December 1941.

Right: Anti-aircraft gunners' Christmas dinner, 1941.

Local Home Guard troops.

damage to windows and walls of 8 houses. The 'all clear' sounded at 00.39 am, 9th December, and anti-aircraft fire during the alerts had been reported as very heavy.

The next raid took place just before Christmas, on Saturday, 20th December, and appeared to be an almost carbon copy of the raid of 11th September. An early evening raid, the siren sounding at 5.24 pm, the 'all clear' at 6.05 pm.

Just seconds after the siren sounded, Special Constable Harrop, who was on duty at the sea banks between the Sand and Gravel Company and Hendon gas works, when he heard an aircraft approaching from the sea. Soon after, Harrop caught sight of the aircraft flying from the direction of Ryhope at a height of about 50 feet. White lights were showing on the starboard wing and in the centre of the fuselage. Harrop mentioned in his report that he thought that the planes was one of ours, due to the lights showing: 'As I watched, it climbed up and flew over the cliffs in between the Grangetown Swimming Club and the Rocket House. He turned right and flew along the railway line in the direction of the gas works, when it seemed to be over the gas works he released two bombs. The aircraft immediately turned seaward. Both bombs exploded close to each other in the St Thomas' Allotments (Robinson Terrace and close to Hendon gas works) 100 yards south of the American Oil Depot, making a large crater 90 feet long by 50 feet wide and 15 to 20 feet deep. The west side of the LNER dock railway line was damaged and blocked by debris, but this did not interfere with traffic on the other 2 sets of tracks.

Seventeen houses nearby suffered damage to roofs from lumps of clay thrown up by the blast. The only casualty was a 12-year-old boy who had a suspected broken leg and was taken to the Royal Infirmary.

By the end of 1941, Britain no longer stood alone. Backed now by powerful allies, Russia and United States, the odds were, perhaps slowly at first, being steadily stacked against the Axis Forces.

THE TIDE TURNS
1942

Fulwell Fire Station extensively damaged only days after being officially opened.

The first raid of the New Year came on Thursday, 15th January, the sirens sounding at 5.46pm. At 5.55 pm an aircraft was seen flying from south to north at low altitude, dropping 4 bombs, 50 to 60 feet apart, in Backhouse Park. The aircraft was reported to have been flying low across town, machine-gunning as it made its escape. Many people collected spent bullets and cartridges cases. All the bombs exploded causing earth, trees, branches and various shrubbery to be thrown on to the west side of Ryhope Road, blocking the road for about 300 hundred yards. In one of the craters gas and water pipes were damaged and electric cables exposed. Overhead tram lines had also been damaged. Some nearby buildings also sustained damage including Backhouse Park Lodge, Hendon Hill House, The Synagogue in Ryhope Road, The Cedars garage and houses in The Cedars. The Art School had 130 panes of glass smashed and there was slight damage to Christ Church and the vestry roof. Three people were slightly hurt. North and southbound traffic was diverted for about 40 minutes until Ryhope Road had been cleared. The all-clear sounded at 6.26 pm.

There was a respite of almost 4 months before the next bombs fell on the town. The sirens sounded at 2.34 am, Friday, 1st May. Four bombs were dropped, at 2.59 am, east of the LNER Sunderland to Newcastle line south of Sea Road, Fulwell. On duty in Atkinson Road was police Inspector McDonald, who heard the bombs falling, and immediately after the detonations described: 'The whole neighbourhood covered with debris.'

In their shelter, in the back garden of 26 Mayswood Road, were John (48) and Edith Swaddle (48), when a bomb, estimated as a 500kg bomb, exploded close to the shelter, trapping them in the rubble. The Swaddle's son, Leonard, escaped because he hadn't gone to the shelter with his parents when the warning had sounded. He told the *Sunderland Echo*: 'I stayed in bed for a while, then I got up and got dressed. I heard my mother shout from the shelter "Is Len there?" I answered "Yes" and shouted I was going upstairs for a scarf. I was coming down again fastening the scarf around my neck when I heard the squeal of the bomb dropping. I scrambled down the stairs and flung myself into a cupboard at the bottom of the stairs as the bomb fell. My first thought was to get to the shelter, but I found my way blocked by a shed which had been wrecked. I climbed out of the kitchen window and saw that the shelter had been wrecked too and I knew it was a bad job.'

Rescue parties soon recovered the bodies of Len's parents, both had been killed instantly. 'It was a strong shelter which my father, who is a fitter, had made himself out of heavy baulks of timber

26 Mayswood Road, Fulwell, where a husband and wife were killed in their shelter.

and steel plates, built almost underground, but no matter what type of shelter they had been in at that spot they could hardly have escaped, so close did the bomb fall.'

Another bomb fell on the nearby Fulwell Fire Station which had only been officially opened on 7th April. Part of the station was demolished, by a bomb, again estimated as 500kg.

Fulwell Club & Institute damaged at the same time as the Fire Station.

A group of firemen in the station yard had flung themselves to the ground when they heard the bombs falling and descending the stairs inside the building was fireman Walter Sharpen, who was buried in the debris. Colleagues rushed to his aid and quickly dug him out.

Hetty Rodgers was taking a routine call at her switchboard in the fire station, when the bomb exploded, but would not leave her post. For her courageous act she was mentioned in dispatches and later awarded the Empire Medal.

The third bomb, estimated as a 250kg, demolished the Fulwell Social Club & Institute, where the steward, on fire-watching duty, standing at the kitchen door and his wife in the kitchen, flung themselves to the floor when they heard the bombs coming. The couple escaped injury despite being hit by debris and covered in dust.

The fourth bomb fell in Ferry's farmyard, killing a pony that was used for a milk round, and some chickens. Some day old chicks escaped even though their coop was in the middle of the yard and the blast lifted a heavy cart over the coop.

The next raid on the town saw the Luftwaffe have one of their most successful raids to date, in terms of damage to the war effort. The sirens sounded at 1.31 am. At 1.50 am, bombs were heard falling close to the river Wear, about three-quarters of a mile up river from Wearmouth Bridge. No explosions were heard and it was assumed that the bombs had fallen in the river, as a search of the area revealed no damage.

It was not until 8.05 am, with the Luftwaffe crews back at the base, relaxing after the night's long mission over the North Sea, when their handiwork began to pay dividends. One of the bombs exploded in the river, causing serious damage to the stern of the SS *Zealous* and slight damage to the bow of the SS *Empire Ford*, both of which were tied up opposite Hetton Staithes. One of the bombs had actually hit the *Empire Ford's* bow before entering the river.

The captain of the *Zealous*, attempted to move the ship from alongside the *Empire Ford*, his aim to take his vessel closer to the quay, as water was entering the ship through damaged plates. As this was taking place, at 8.17 am a second bomb exploded, again in the river causing further damage to the

The Zealous listing after she was damaged by 2 delayed action bombs that had fallen in the river during the night of 5th June.

Zealous and she started to settle by the stern.

PC J.S. Richardson, who was on board giving assistance to casualties from the first explosion, had already called for ambulance services and to the fire service for water pumping equipment and for the fireboat, the *Fire Queen* to be brought up. Seven members of the crew of the *Zealous* and one on the *Empire Ford* were wounded and taken to the Royal Infirmary.

Another search for bombs on land turned up 2 further unexploded bombs, one on the Rock Top allotments and the other about 20 yards away embedded in the embankment of one of the staithes railways. These caused a halt to the loading at Lambton, Hetton and Joicey Colliery Staithes. Also, being only 80 yards from the power station, the town's electricity supply was in jeopardy.

At 11.28 am Lieutenant Cyril Punt of Leamside and Sub-Lieutenant Charles Gill of Cornwall, both of the Royal Navy Volunteer Reserve, based at Grand Hotel, Sunderland, examined the bombs and had confirmed they were not mines. The officers were about 20 yards from the crater, in the allotments, on the steps down to the staithes, when the bomb exploded.

Punt reported: 'We dropped to the ground and a good deal of debris fell on top of us. Part of a railway sleeper fell near to us, and I think this must have caused the injuries to Gill.' Gill suffered a broken leg and ribs, and Punt injuries to his shoulder. Also hurt were Police Sergeants Tait and Bird and PC Taylor, a bomb disposal officer and a private soldier.

On 18th June, it was reported to the ARP Committee that one uxb remained and its exact location had not been traced. The Bomb Disposal Section decided that the bomb could not be found and closed the incident.

There was further respite before the next bombs fell in the district. The sirens sounded at 10.46 pm, Friday, 28th August. At 11.15 pm, an aircraft, travelling from north-east to south-west, dropped 8 phosphourus incendiary bombs, similar in size to the 50kg high explosive bomb. All the bombs fell in Fulwell Quarry covering an area of about 150 yards. There was no damage, and all the bombs burnt themselves out in the small craters they made. The all-clear sounded at 0.13 am, Saturday the 29th.

Nine days later, at 11.15 pm, Sunday, 6th September, 'Purple' warning was received and 'Red' at 11.39 pm. Ten minutes after the siren had sounded heavy anti-aircraft fire was seen to the north and south of the town.

Fifteen minutes after midnight, Thornholme was informed that a projectile had fallen at the junction of Alexandra Road and Langport Drive. Two pieces of metal tail fin were found in the small crater, which damaged the footpath. Later that morning a further report was made of a piece of metal, with a similar fin, had fallen through the roof of a house in Louis Avenue, on the north side of the river. Metal and fins were later identified by a bomb disposal officer as anti-aircraft ammunition.

Again there was a brief interlude between bombing raids over Wearside, but the next raid, on Sunday, 11th October was an altogether more serious affair. 'Purple' warning was received at 9.00 pm, the sirens sounding five minutes later and the alert ended at 10.07 pm.

At 9.15 pm, high explosive bombs fell in the Hendon area, the largest of which, estimated at 1000kg, fell in the centre of Corporation Road, about 50 yards south of Villette Road, making a crater the width of the road and setting fire to a gas main. Damage was extensive.

Nos 3 to 11 Corporation Road, all houses, were demolished as were Nos 2, 4, 6 and 8 Villette Road, all shops. The west wing of Hendon Valley Road School was badly damaged as was St Cecilia's Church.

Summoned to the devastation was Chief Officer Rescue Services J. Goldsmith from Barley Mow Depot, who was initially informed that two people were trapped at some corner shops, but he only managed to find a cat

A large bomb caused many casualties and extensive damage to the area around Corporation Road and Villette Road, during a raid on 11th October.

and dog. Going to No 5 Corporation Road, Goldsmith again was told of two people being trapped. A colleague, A. Lackenby noticed some movement amongst the wreckage which turned out to be a man's knee. Goldsmith wrote in his report: 'We set to work to extricate him which was no rush job, but a job of patience and careful handling on account of the very great possibility of a fall of debris, in which case the casualty could have been reburied.'

The bomb which fell in the middle of Corporation Road, burst gas and water mains, leaving a water-filled crater.

The man being rescued was Mr B. Nottingham (52), who was seemingly uninjured, thanking those who had rescued him. However, he was taken to hospital where it was found he had fractured ribs. Mr Nottingham told his rescuers that at the time of the explosion he was coming downstairs with his wife and that she could be found around the same position he was discovered. After a further search amongst the rubble, Mrs Agnes Nottingham (46) was recovered, but she had been killed.

In Canon Cockin Street, Mrs Weir, her husband, their daughter Mrs Mason and her daughter Olive (6) were in two minds as to go to the shelter or not.

Hendon Valley Road school was also badly damaged.

Mrs Weir told the *Sunderland Echo*: 'We were wondering whether to go into the shelter in the yard when we heard a plane overhead and made a dash for it. We had just got in when there was a terrific crash and we heard the roof of the house being smashed in. Great lumps of stone crashed all around us, but we all escaped without a scratch.'

The Millers next door were not so lucky, not being able to get to their refuge in time. Mrs Weir went on: 'We heard their house come down and the little girl Gwendoline Miller (12) ran out covered in blood and crying "Ernie is buried." An RAF man who was in the street ran into the ruins and carried out Ernie (her brother), but he had been killed having been blown from one end of the kitchen to the other.

On fire-watching duty in a Christian Spiritualist Church above shops on a corner of a main road (probably Villette Road) was Mrs Sarah Lister and her daughter Mrs Elliott. Mrs Lister said: 'Things got pretty hot and we went downstairs and stood in the doorway. We heard a bomb coming down and the blast blew us backwards up the stairs.' Mrs Lister suffered a cut to the head. The church was completely wrecked except for the staircase. Mrs Lister's husband, John (71), was at their home at 10 Corporation Road and was seriously injured.

Fred Blackburn was on his way home when he heard the bomb falling. Unable to get to the front door of his house for flames he went around the back and found the front of the house demolished. His wife and daughter were safe in their shelter, but his son Fred (19) was in the kitchen and was hurt about the shoulders when trapped in a doorway.

At 3 Corporation Road, lived picture house manager James Beattie and his wife Elizabeth. They were slightly injured and their house wrecked. Mr Beattie had been in a cinema a year earlier when it was hit by a bomb, but on that occasion he was unhurt. The next morning the Beatties' dog 'Flash' was photographed by the *Echo* on a pillow amongst the wreckage. Others that lost their lives were at 7 Corporation Road, Thomas (56) and Alice (52) Stoker and four-year-old June Wilson of No 6 and Sarah Terena Colvin (55) of No 11 and Joan Doyle (16), of 6 Hyde Street. A further 75 people were injured.

The Germans also dropped a number of Firepots (a 50kg HE bomb case filled with incendiary materials), 8 in total being reported. One exploded at 29 Tower Street, which was demolished and another came to earth at 42 Back Tower Street. At 42 Thompson Street a bomb fell in the backyard causing extensive damage.

Unexploded bombs fell at 22 Athol Road, under the front bay window, and at No 44 where the bomb crashed through the roof and on to the kitchen floor. Athol Road was closed to traffic while the bombs were defused.

At Nos 12 and 25 Hendon Burn Avenue, bombs fell in the front gardens and again the road was closed. Several roads were closed due to a bomb in South Back Ward Street. Those who had to be evacuated while uxb's were dealt with went to friends or were accommodated at the Hendon Board School.

It was reported that another bomb fell into the sea close to the British Oil Store at South Dock, and an unexploded anti-aircraft shell dropped in Neale Street, Fulwell.

The following day the German News Agency stated that Sunderland was raided, bombers operating from a height of 2,200 ft. The report, which was quoted in the *Sunderland Echo*, went on: 'Numerous anti-aircraft batteries immediately opened fire over the harbour area. The German bombers, however, flew over the shipbuilding yards to other important objectives in the town and harbour districts. All the bombers returned to their bases after the raid, which lasted nearly an hour'.

The next bombs to fall on Sunderland were on Friday, 16th October. At 9.35 pm 'Purple' warning was received and the sirens sounded just 5 minutes later. Ten minutes after the purple warning, Police reported to Thornholme that an enemy aircraft which had been caught in searchlight beams, had been shot down and had fallen in flames into the sea, this being witnessed by numerous people.

At 10.02 pm there was a heavy concentration of anti-aircraft fire followed by 3 bombs falling on the south-east central portion of the town, 2 of which exploded, killing 14 people.

The first bomb fell on or near to 6 and 7 Tatham Street, trapping 2 families, the Cooks and the Halversons and damaging the Education Architects' Department Feeding Centre (or kitchen) and a tram.

On fire-watching duty at the Feeding Centre, was Robert Leadbitter, who watched the bomber being shot down before returning indoors for a cup of tea. Minutes later the bombs fell. Rescue worker William Hall told the *Sunderland Echo*: 'I was off duty and in my house when the bombs dropped. I dashed along the street and was told there was people buried. We started to dig and very soon we were able to get out three fire-watchers. Two were obviously dead and the third seemed to be beyond help.' Robert Leadbitter was one of those killed.

At 1.52 am, Saturday the 17th, it was reported to the Incident Post, which had been set up at the Crown Buildings, Tatham Street, that 9 people were not accounted for at 6 and 7 Tatham Street and a further 3 at No 58. However, those from 58 were located safe soon after the report was made.

At 9.11 am Brian Monagahn (29) of Hastings Street, on duty as a

6 & 7 Tatham Street, Hendon, demolished by a direct hit, during the 16th October raid.

fire-watcher at the Education Architects Department, was reported missing by his father. It was later confirmed that he had been killed.

At 1.43 pm the body of 15-year-old James William Landers, of Ann Street was identified.

It wasn't until 3.50 pm, almost 18 hours after the bomb had fallen, that the first body was recovered from the devastation of 6 Tatham Street and not until 1.10 am Sunday the 18th that it was reported that the bodies of a woman and two children were recovered from No 7.

Killed were Mrs Mary Ann Cook (or Wardle) (42), her daughters Joyce (11), Margaret Rose (5), Doreen (3) and 6-month-old Gwendline, and at this incident Diana Marion Borreson (2) of Murton Street. All the victims had been killed instantly, some appeared to have been in their beds. Shelters at the rear of the houses were virtually undamaged.

John George Halverson, a picture house manager, was walking towards his house, 7 Tatham Street, when the bomb fell. He ran to his house to find it demolished and his wife, Ida (45) and daughter Eileen (13) and step father Septimus Carter (73) trapped in the rubble. All three were killed.

The second bomb fell at the east end of Tavistock Place, demolishing Moore's food warehouse and garage. Some residential property was seriously damaged, some of which had already been blitzed in the raid of 15th April 1941. A considerable amount of food was destroyed by fire, which took almost an hour to extinguish.

Fire-watchers at Moore's Warehouse were more fortunate. Company secretary Mr E. Heslop was with two other members of staff: 'It was lucky for us that we were at the opposite end of the building from where the garage was situated. We were in a passage when we heard the bomb falling. We dived to

Moore's Warehouse in Tavistock Place, close to the Tatham Street incident, was also demolished, destroying large quantities of food.

The Mayor of Sunderland, Councillor Myers Wayman inspects a Valentine Tank in Sunderland, March 1942.

the floor and had hardly got there when the whole building seemed to go up.'

The third bomb, a 1000kg, fell in Laura Street, at the junction with Tavistock Place, but thankfully did not explode. Other fatalities were Walter Devonport (64), of 56 Tatham Street and Edward Carter (50), of Robinson Terrace. Gas, Water and electric supplies were all affected. At 10.00 pm an unexploded anti-aircraft shell fell in the back garden of 11 Nawton Avenue, off Newcastle Road. The 'all-clear' sounded at 10.24 pm.

On Saturday, 12th December, 'Purple' warning was received at 4.45 am, the sirens sounding just three minutes later. During the alert, which lasted until 5.52 am, 2 anti-aircraft shells returned to earth intact. The first crashed through the north-side gable end of 31 Mere Knolls Road, Fulwell, a newsagent's shop. The shell then exploded causing extensive damage to fittings and to stock. Plate glass windows were blown out and outside wall perforated by shell splinters. Some windows in surrounding property were also smashed.

At 14 Stratford Avenue, Grangetown, a shell had landed in the soft earth in the rear garden. The shell had not exploded and was later found at a depth of 9 feet 6 inches.

A German communique dealing with the raids referred to: 'Extensive fires and destruction wrought by waves of bombers at Sunderland.'

The force overhead had been only 10 aircraft and although flares were dropped at Sunderland, the town was not bombed.

Another Christmas, another New Year, the fourth of the war. The Germans were soon to find themselves retreating on all fronts and in the midst of one of those severe Russian winters, General Von Paulus was busy surrendering half a million men into Soviet captivity at Stalingrad.

THE LAST ONSLAUGHT
1943

The Jack Crawford Hotel in Waterloo Place, Monkwearmouth, after the raid of 24th May 1943.

At 7.43 pm on Wednesday, 13th January, the sirens sounded. The all-clear being an hour and 3 minutes later.

Around 8.25 pm, aircraft were heard approaching the town from a northerly direction and soon afterwards 8 bombs fell around South Dock. Two were 1000kg high explosive, 4 were Firepots and 2 phosphorus oil.

The first HE fell on the LNER Railway, 100 yards south of the engine sheds and immediately west of the South Dock. Extensive damage was caused to 2 sidings and some loaded wagons, one of which was full of British 2 inch mortar bombs. These were hurled in all directions, some landing as far away as the Town Moor. The second bomb fell on the same railway, 150 yards south of the first bomb, but only caused damage to a surrounding wall.

The first of the Firepots fell on the railway at the foot of Barrack Street approach to the South Docks, damaging three tracks. The second fell near to the railway bridge, in the garden of Nos 1 & 2 Railway Terrace, immediately west of Hendon Dock, doing little damage. The third fell at the base of the steam house chimney of Monsanto Chemical Works demolishing the fan-house, causing a small fire which was soon extinguished. The fourth fell on the LNER Railway Londonderry Junction, between the main lines, but caused no damage.

Of the phosphorus bombs, the first fell on the east quay of the South Dock, again causing a small fire. and the second dropped at the north end of South Dock, on the west quay.

Damage to buildings during the bombing was restricted to a few broken windows, mainly to housing around the Town Moor.

The only casualty was Mary Ann Simpson (80) who was hurt when a ceiling collapsed in the house in which she was sheltering at 12 Mary Street, Southwick, during a period of intense gunfire during the raid.

On Wednesday, 3rd February, the 'Red' warning was received at 8.19 pm, the all-clear sounding just under an hour later at 9.08 pm.

Twenty minutes after the siren had sounded, an aircraft, travelling south-east, was caught in searchlight beams. The aircraft was immediately engaged by anti-aircraft batteries and what appeared to be a string of white lights were seen, falling from the aeroplane. At the same time, a single HE bomb was dropped, presumably by the same aircraft, which pierced the concrete roadway of the South Dock, 60 feet from the north-west corner of Hendon Dock.

The bomb, estimated as 500kg, later exploded at 4.50 am, Thursday the 4th, making a crater 31 feet in diameter, which immediately filled with water. Extensive damage was done to No 31 Staith by pieces of concrete, and to a military blockhouse, which measured 18 feet by 17 feet by 9 feet, positioned roughly 5 yards from the bomb entry point, which was lifted bodily and came to rest on the lip of the crater. The crew of the SS *Elizabeth Lysaght* which was lying 30 yards from the entry point, alongside the quay at Hendon Dock, taking on coal from 31 Staith, had to be evacuated, but the ship suffered no damage. Two gas company employees, working some distance from the bomb were injured by debris. For a time, there were restrictions to coal loading at 31 Staith and to shipping in Hendon Dock and a small refining factory was closed.

The night of Thursday 11th and early morning of Friday, 12th March was another night of rogue anti-aircraft shells, this time with tragic consequences. 'Red' warning was at 9.42 pm and the all-clear sounded at 10,47 pm. Sirens were again sounded at 11.19 pm, the all-clear at 00.13 am.

At 10.08 pm an anti-aircraft shell fell at the junction of Whitburn Street and Dundas Street, breaking windows of 3 houses. At 10.40 pm, another shell exploded on contact with the roof girders of the Wheatsheaf tram sheds, damaging 6 trams, mainly broken windows. Around the same time another shell fell in the back yard of a house in Dundas Street, near to the tram sheds.

Between the times of these shells returning to earth, 2 further shells fell on Durham Road, at 10.15 pm, one in the grounds of the Children's Hospital, and the other in the front garden of a house, on the opposite side of the road from the hospital. Both these shells exploded, the latter one causing serious damage to glass and woodwork of 3 houses and killing Mrs Elizabeth Nicholson (59) of 22 Humbledon View, who was at the entrance of her home.

Two others, William Graham (54) and Andrew Coughlin (68) also suffered injures from shell splinters.

These incidents followed a warning given by Herbert Morrison, Minister for Home Security, made days previously, regarding the dangers of people being caught out or standing out in the open during air raids.

On Sunday, 14th March, 'Purple' warning was received at 11.00 pm, the sirens sounding 6 minutes later. The all-clear brought relief just over an hour later at 00.15 am, Monday the 15th.

From 11.15 pm enemy aircraft commenced to drop parachute flares followed by Firepots which fell in Otto Terrace. Soon afterwards another stick of Firepots fell at between John Candlish Road and Hylton Street. Minutes later a third stick of Firepots dropped between The Cedars to Thornhill. Altogether 30 Firepots landed, 5 of which failed to ignite, causing extensive damage to 2 schools and about 40 houses.

Then at 11.45 pm, parachute mines made an unwelcome return to Sunderland, when 2 floated into the town centre, in St Thomas Street and in Union Street. The crater made in Union Street was 40 feet wide by 10 feet deep.

On duty as a fire watcher at Book's fashion shop in Crowtree Road was Solomon Freedman, who witnessed the descent of the mine above the Railway

Devastation caused by a parachute mine in Union Street.

Station and Union Street and pointed this out to PC Harry Peart, who was at his post at Holmeside Corner. Peart ran along Crowtree Road in an attempt to take cover. Seconds later he saw: 'The mine explode with an orange glow above White's Market.'

The blast threw Peart to the ground and he was hit around the head by debris. Recovering, he made his way towards the market and came to the Empress Hotel in Union Street. The hotel had been partially demolished, and the force of the explosion had moved the hotel 6 inches along its foundations.

PC Peart, on hearing cries for help from the upper part of the shattered building, searched for a suitable entrance to get to those trapped.

By this time, others were already beginning to enter the Hotel. Head warden Benjamin Blacker, was on duty at his post at 22C Cumberland Street, entered the Hotel through the Union Street entrance, along with a civilian named T. Hope. The men climbed the staircase to the first floor and found Home Guard Officer George Greenshields, already working to free those trapped.

Greenshields who was in Crowtree Road, about to go on duty, when the mine exploded, later recalled: 'The flash, the noise and blast were terrific.'

Recounting for the *Sunderland Echo*: he said: 'I ran down Northumberland Street into a cloud of dust and falling debris.' Joined by a civilian, they heard cries for help coming from a wrecked house near the bottom of Northumberland Street, and they managed to carry people out and into houses less damaged nearby: 'Then we went down to the wreck of the Empress Hotel. It was a terrible sight. About half of the hotel had been blown away and was just a heap of rubble in the road.' The pair managed to force a way through a partially blocked door and extricated the manageress from behind the reception desk. Despite her injuries and being in a state of shock, she gave her rescuers information as to the location of others in the building.

Greenshields went on: 'We scrambled up the remains of a fire escape and into what was left of a passage on the second floor. All the rooms on one side of the passage had just disappeared, and it was difficult to tell where the remaining rooms were, so great was the destruction. We scrambled into one room through what I thought was a window, examining the place in daylight I see it was an almost blocked up door.'

They found a WAAF officer, dressed in her greatcoat over her nightwear and she insisted on helping the rescuers, holding a torch while they dug for victims.

The rescuers were then joined by 2 more policemen, PCs Harvey and Turnbull, who had climbed into a partially demolished room, the floor of which was hanging over the crater. Warden Blacker then passed 6 people they had released from debris, through a hole in a wall, about 3 feet in diameter, one of whom was bleeding heavily and badly injured. PC Harvey then carried them across to another window and passed them onto PC Turnbull before being carried into a hallway by PC Peart. They were then put onto a commandeered haulage contractors van, which took them to the Royal Infirmary.

PC Turnbull was full of praise for the civilians who had assisted in the rescue work, stating that they: 'carried out a splendid piece of work, having regard to the fact that had the floor of the room in which they were working collapsed, they would have been thrown into the bomb crater a considerable distance below. There was also a great probability of the remainder of the roof collapsing.'

Alfred William Tyrer (63) of London, stage director of the aptly titled *Damaged Goods* which was showing at the Empire Theatre, was knocked unconscious by the ceiling of his hotel room collapsing on top of him and his wife Gladwyn. Arthur Rowntree (47), of Farnham Terrace, Sunderland, Edward Halliday (64), of London and seaman Matthew Blair all received treatment.

Property surrounding the hotel and White's Market was a scene of devastation. Fire-watcher Ralph Morrison (59) was killed while on duty at White's Market.

This mine also claimed the lives of fire-watchers William Walton (57) of Elvington Street, Fulwell and Alfred Munro (16) of Marion Street, both killed on duty at Young's Garage in South Street.

The second mine fell at St Thomas Street and John Street, demolishing the 113-year-old St Thomas' Church, killing the Rev Leyland Orton (58), on duty as a fire watcher. First policeman on the scene was Special Sergeant J.E.G. Chapman, who described: 'a cloud of smoke and dust which hung over the scene was so thick that it was literally impossible to see what had happened for some time.'

Initially listed as missing, Rev Orton was thought to have been near to the entrance of the church or talking to other fire watchers at the Baltic Chambers, when both church and office block were wrecked. Mrs Orton and their son David (20), were sheltering in the vicarage, which was also badly damaged, but both were unhurt. David appealed to Sergeant Chapman for help in locating his father and both attempted to get through the mass of debris in John Street but they found it impossible without the proper equipment.

Chapman then went to the aid of a woman, trapped in her house in John Street: 'When I carried her to the door, she insisted in going back for her pet dog and then for her false teeth which she found undamaged in a glass in a cupboard amongst the rubble.'

A mine destroyed St Thomas' Church.

John Street, opposite St Thomas' Church.

Fire-watcher Ernest Johnson (16) of Peebles Road was killed on duty at the Baltic Chambers.

Joseph Murtha, another fire guard on duty near to where the mine fell, was found by wardens and ambulancemen in a corner of a room, at the Engineers' Department in the River Wear Commissioners building in St Thomas Street with serious facial injuries and died on his way to hospital. Two colleagues, Miss Skinner and Miss Gettings were making for the shelter when the mine exploded, and were blown down a flight of stairs. Damage to the town centre was immense from both mines.

Then at 11.50 pm, 2 further mines fell in Nora Street, High Barnes and in Seaforth Road, Humbledon Hill. The first of these mines fell at Back Nora Street and West Back Colchester Terrace. The police incident post was set up at Smythes bakery in Cleveland Road, then later moved to the Police Box in Kayll Road, as all the phones went dead.

It was at this incident that the most casualties occurred, although details are scarce as to what exactly happened.

At 2 Nora Street, Mrs Mary Bewley (50) lost her life as did Henry Durrant (65), of No 5 and Miss Catherine Moorhead (73) of No 6. Other fatalities were at 207 Cleveland Road where Mrs Jane Eleanor Cromie (66) and Ella Riley (50) were killed and 50-year-old Willaim Dixon was killed at 68 Colchester Terrace.

A few people had narrow escapes, none more so than 90-year-old George Bathgate, who together with his daughter-in-law went into their surface shelter at their home at 211 Cleveland Road. The explosion wrecked the house and the shelter. 'It (the shelter) seemed to split. Debris was flying in my face.,' recalled Mr Bathgate to the *Sunderland Echo*. He went on: 'Then we found that a wall had been blown out and half the concrete roof had fallen down ... into the shelter without touching either of us. My daughter-in-law crawled out over the broken roof, I handed out the dog and then she helped me to crawl out.'

The fourth mine of the raid, at Seaforth Road, caused much devastation, but almost unbelievably, there were no deaths. Only one person was injured.

All the houses in Seaforth

The remains of a tree, blasted on to the roof of a house in Durham Road.

More destruction, at Colchester Terrace and Nora Street, High Barnes, again by a parachute mine.

Mr & Mrs Rose in the ruins of their home, 2-3 Seaforth Road, Humbledon. The Rose family and their neighbours were in a Morrison table shelter.

Road and half those in Humbledon Park suffered varying degrees of damage and windows were broken over a much wider area.

It was initially feared that 2 families were trapped in an Anderson shelter at 3 Seaforth Road. Both this house and the adjoining semi-detatced house were both demolished.

What follows is taken from an account especially written for the Northern Civil Defence Region:

'Widow, 55-year-old Edith Bennett and her school teacher daughter Miss Phyllis Bennett (29), lived with an aunt, Miss Mabel Carney (8) at 2 Seaforth Road. In the adjoining house were Mr David Rose (62) his wife and son Maurice (29).

On this occasion Mr Bennett decided to take up the offer from Mr Rose to share their Morrison table shelter, which was situated in the Roses' dining room. After everyone had taken up their positions, the wire netted sides were fitted into place.

No sooner had they settled down, when they heard the drone of an enemy aircraft overhead. They suddenly felt the shelter and themselves being lifted for some height and then dropped. Then they saw the flash of the explosion before quantities of masonry thundered down on top of the shelter. The force and weight of the debris had bent the shelter's steel legs and the pressure had forced the protective wire sides and ends into such a state as to cramp the occupants into half the original space.

After what seemed to them an eternity, but only a few minutes in reality, the Rescue Services arrived and they shouted their whereabouts to them. After about half an hour's digging the rescuers made a small passage down through tons of masonry, to the side of the shelter and one by one they were carefully extricated.

All were in a state of shock. Mr Rose, having been trapped by his feet, was bruised and Mrs Bennett had bruising to her back, but both were allowed home after hospital treatment. The edge of the crater was only a few feet away from the dining room which contained the shelter.'

Nurses clearing up after blast damaged the Children's Hospital on Durham Road, on the 14th March 1943.

Under fire, and damaged again, was the Children's Hospital in Durham Road and although windows were shattered and plaster from ceilings in the wards fell onto beds, no-one was hurt. About 50 patients, some seriously ill, were wrapped in blankets by nursing staff and helpers and taken to shelters then evacuated to other hospitals in the town.

A Sister recalled to the *Sunderland Echo* the following day: 'It is a miracle that none of us were killed or injured.'

Describing the detonation of the mine, she went on to say: 'Suddenly there was a flash and a roar, and the ceilings and windows came in on us. We dashed around in the darkness, lifting shattered window frames and pieces of glass off the beds. The children were absolutely marvellous. Some of them sang and joked in the shelters.'

A small fire broke out in one of the rooms, but was soon extinguished.

Thirty Firepots caused serious damage to about 40 houses, Diamond Hall Infants School and Barnes, Chester Road and Bede Schools.

Damage in the town was so bad that the civil defence services

Cornice stone flung into Fawcett Street by blast.

Clearing up in Fawcett Street, a photograph not passed by the censor at the time.

were swamped with the task of clearing up and army units were drafted in to help. Teams from South Shields were in Sunderland for a week.

One hundred and fifty three people were made homeless, and were housed in 4 rest centres and all had been temporarily rehoused within 24 hours. Eventually, 1,100 people had to be billeted while repairs to the homes could be carried out. Sixteen people were killed and around 100 injured, 31 seriously.

A week later, the raiders were back, on Monday, 22nd March, the sirens sounding at 10.48 pm. The echoes of the sirens had hardly faded when around 240 incendiary bombs were dropped in the Southwick District.

On duty in Collingwood Street was Sergeant Robinson when he saw a blinding flash and heard something crash to the ground in Edward Burdis Street. He saw that incendiaries were burning over a distance of 20 yards and that 2 houses were on fire. All the bombs were extinguished by the street fire watchers. Three people were slightly hurt and 71 Edward Burdis Street, occupied by Mrs Ethel Brown (51), Olive Brown (18), and Rita Poulton (19), was burnt out. There was slight damage at Nos 66, 69 and 70.

More serious was at 11.12 pm when two high explosive bombs, thought to be 500kg, fell in the marshalling railway siding next to the railway sheds north-west of South Docks, close to Prospect Row, in the East End. Only one bomb exploded, but caused considerable damage to railway lines, rolling stock and superficial damage to around 150 houses, an ARP store at Prospect House, a public house and the Station Hotel in Prospect Row. Two people were injured. Prospect Row was blocked to traffic from Silver Street to Chapel Street.

Buildings damaged included St John's Church and School in Prospect Row, together with the canteen and 11 houses and shops, Lyons garage in South Docks, four houses in Chapel Street, Moor Board School, three houses in Stafford Street, Nos 3 to 34 Moorgate Street, Hartley Street Mission with 9 houses, 10 houses in Silver Street, 11 in Barrack Street, 18 houses in Harrison's

Buildings, one house in High Street East, 60 homes in Burleigh Garth, one in Warren Street, St John's Vicarage, Trinity Place, St Patrick's Vicarage and Sunderland Parish Church and Vicarage. All this from a single bomb.

A uxb landed about 55 yards south of the other bomb, at No 10 LNER Railway sidings, 100 yards south of Silver Street. BDO Lieutenant Brooke identified the bomb as 1000kg, and it was only 2 feet below the surface. The bomb was defused and cleared by 4.30 pm.

The all-clear sounded exactly an hour after the sirens had sounded, at 11.48 pm.

There was a lull of almost 2 months before the Germans next raid, when on Sunday, 16th May, 127 HE bombs and mines, plus around 1,300 incendiaries fell on the town, killing 69 people. Thirty of the bombs didn't explode, but if they had, fatalities may have numbered into hundreds. 'Purple' warning was received at 1.40 am and 4 minutes later the sirens were sounded.

Many folk had barely time to rouse themselves from beds, dress and get to their shelters before the bombers had arrived, the first dropping flares to guide others.

From records, it appears that the initial stick of bombs fell at 1.58 am and landed at Nos 25$^{1}/_{2}$, 28/29 Back Alexandra Park, another in a field behind 27 Alexandra Park and two that failed to detonate, at 7 Belle Vue Park and at the rear of 9 and 11 Otto Terrace. One person, 52-year-old Joseph Taylor, of 35 Alexandra Park, was killed and numerous people were injured. In one of the houses that was badly damaged, a shelter made from a converted steel boiler saved the lives of 3 people.

A water filled crater on the pitch at Roker Park football ground.

Two minutes later, at 2.00 am, a 500kg bomb fell in the front of the Main Stand at Roker Park football ground, another in the club car park in Grantham Road and a 250kg on the car park at the east end of the ground. Patrolling near to the ground

Damage to the Main Stand roof.

Outside Roker Park football ground, where Special Constable Slawther was killed.

was Special Constable Lancelot Slawther (47), who was killed in the blast of one of these bombs, only yards from his home in Beatrice Street. The bombs destroyed the old club house and badly damaged the Sunderland Model Making Works.

Soon afterwards two 1,000kg bombs fell in Oakwood Street, one outside No 15, the other in the road to the west end of the Street. Mercifully neither bomb exploded, it is not difficult to imagine the destruction had they done so. One of the bombs was later found 18 feet below ground.

Others weren't so fortunate. A parachute mine exploded at the junction of Atkinson Road and Rosedale Terrace, Fulwell. Sergeant Rutter was patrolling in Mere Knolls Road when he saw: 'an orange coloured flash and an explosion.'

Rutter found that the mine had come down in the front garden of 88/90 Atkinson Road, demolishing these together with Nos 84 and 86 and that already two Home Guards and a civilian were searching amongst rubble that was No 88, for the Craig family.

After about 15 minutes, James Craig (43) was recovered and first aid immediately administered, but he later died from his injuries. Half an hour later, Mrs Mary Craig (37), was rescued seriously injured, while her sister-in-law Edith Airey (25), had been killed.

During this rescue work, Rutter was informed of the Miller family, next door at No 90, were unaccounted for. The family Anderson shelter was situated on what was now the edge of the large crater. Rutter had seen: 'strewn about Atkinson Road, parts of the Anderson shelter which gave me little hope.'

A party of soldiers were recruited in the efforts to locate the missing family. Around 3.45 am, the Millers were found, all crushed together in the ground, about 10 feet away from the crater and under three or four pieces of shelter. James Miller (47), his wife Gladys (45), and sons Dennis (12), and Gordon (16), Geoffrey (8), and Eric (6), had all died instantly.

Others killed at this incident were Alice Phillips of Sussex, who was staying at 123 Atkinson Road and Robert Goldsmith (54), of Maud Street.

Devastating were the effects of 2 bombs that fell close together, estimated as 1,000kg and a 250kg, in Waterloo Place and Whitburn Street, Monkwearmouth, causing the deaths of 10 people.

Nos 1 to 5 Waterloo Place were completely shattered as were the Jack Crawford Hotel, houses Nos 90 to 94 and the British Restaurant in Whitburn Street. The warden's post situated at the Old School was seriously damaged. There was a small fire in Waterloo Place, but such was the overwhelming requests on the fire service, that an appliance couldn't attended for almost

2 hours after being summoned. Rescue squads from South Shields worked at this incident.

Killed at No 2 Waterloo Place were Mrs Sarah Thwaites (43), and her daughters Evelyn (17) and Mary (10).

Living at 3 Waterloo Place were 2 families, the Laidlers downstairs, and upstairs the Robsons. Twelve-year-old William Robson was with the rest of his family, when, as the raid began they joined the Laidlers' downstairs. There were now 9 people in a single room, Elizabeth Ann Laidler, Thomas (17), Mrs Robson, Jimmy (6), John (5), Katherine (10), Patsy (3) Betty (8 months) and William.

William later wrote an account of the incident after Thomas Laidler's name had been put forward for a bravery award: 'I was sitting in front of the fire with Thomas Laidler beside me, the others were in other parts of the room. Suddenly everything came tumbling down and I was knocked on my back, and a lot of wood and bricks were on top of me. I could not see anything and a big piece of wood across my chest was holding me down. I shouted to Tommy, Are you all right?'

Thomas was trapped with a beam across his back upon which most of the weight of the house was resting. Rescuers had to release everyone else before they attempted to extricate Thomas in case of further collapse.

William recalled: 'A short while later Tommy shouted, "I cannot breath Billy, try and make a hole and get us out, my back is paining." I pulled some stuff away and made a small hole and got some air in. I shouted across to my mother and heard her shouting for someone to get us out. I could hear some men working above us and saw our Jimmy and Johnny crawl out. The men were pulling wood away from us, and the plank was lifted from my chest, I was then able to move and crawled out. The men put me on a stretcher and I was taken away in an ambulance.'

Thomas, fastened tight in the wreckage, unable to see because of dust in his eyes, got a little comfort when one of the rescuers gave him some water.

Rescuers working at Waterloo Place, Monkwearmouth.

Thomas Laidler wrote: 'The Robson children were under the house and they worked to get them out before they started to release me because the house was resting on a beam which was across my back. I think I was there for about three hours before I was got out.' Thomas spent over two weeks in hospital recovering. Patsy (Patricia) Robson and Elizabeth Ann Laidler (52) were killed.

At 4 Waterloo Place, John (10) and Mary (12), Feeney were killed, their parents seriously injured and at No 5, Albert Alcock (53), his wife Emily Jane (50), Mary Alcock (85), and Edward Innins (62), were all killed.

Sheltering in her usual air raid refuge, between the coal house and the outside toilet, was Florence Ann Henderson (50), of 90 Whitburn Street which was situated behind the Jack Crawford Hotel. Mrs Henderson was missing for 3 days before her body was recovered.

At 91 Whitburn Street, Jane Matthew (65), Elizabeth (30) and Gordon Matthew were killed with Eleanor (27) and Henry Taylor (2). The Taylors were apparently alive when rescued but later succumbed to their injuries. At No 92 64-year-old Ellen Matthews and Mary Ethel Swalwell (27) and at No 94 John T. Shovelin also lost their lives.

As the raid progressed either an incendiary or the remains of a flare, ignited oil soaked rubbish next to the oil storage tank at Greenwell's yard in the South Docks. Soon the tank and its contents were ablaze and burning oil was flowing from the dock side onto the water.

The flames provided an excellent target for the Germans, and at least one aircraft fired cannon shells at the tank. It was not long before over 600 tons of oil was blazing.

Added to this, three HE bombs had been dropped, two of which fell into the river, one about 30 feet north-west of the *Fire Queen*, the other abreast of the tugboat *Wexford* which was lying at the buoys below the *Fire Queen*. The third bomb fell on Austin's sawmill, situated at the east end of Austin's Shipyard, also damaging the Scotia Marine Works.

The punctured oil tanks at Greenwell's Yard, South Docks.

Two men from the *Wexford* were injured, Abraham Dixon (79), of Dundas Street who died from his wounds and Thomas Kirtley (60) was seriously injured. Other tugs, *Seaburn*, *President* and *Snowdon* all sustained damage from what appeared to be cannon fire.

Sub Inspector James Pennington arrived at the river station at 2.45 am and found the station and boats badly damaged. Steam was billowing from the *Fire Queen's* boiler. Helped by PC Hunter they managed to put out the fire and once the steam had cleared they found a large hole and dents in the boiler and damaged pipes. The hull was holed in places, but was in no danger of sinking.

Pennington and other policemen experienced great difficulty in starting the motor of the *Fire Queen* to enable them to get to the fire at Greenwell's. Once started however, they made their way towards the blaze but found the way blocked by the burning fuel.

The men, Pennington, three sergeants and 11 constables landed at Corporation Quay and ran to the fireboat *Fire King*. Steam was raised and on instruction from the dock master Captain Chapman, were ordered to make for the Clock Corner, Hudson Dock. This was at 4.45 am. Captain Chapman raised the dock gates to allow the *Fire King* into the dock basin, and was tied up alongside the outer gates. Pumping commenced with four jets. Fire floats and boats from all over the Wear were called to help tackle the fire and several vessels were damaged in containing the inferno. As dawn came the oil tank finally collapsed sending a column of flames high into the sky. The fire was eventually extinguished at 7.00 am.

Back on land, a parachute mine had fallen to the east side of Fulwell Crossing, at around 2.15 am. Destruction was severe and widespread, but amazingly no one was killed. Bryant Wise (20), of 3 Vivian Square and George Peel, of Railway Cottages, were seriously injured. Houses at Nos 117, 127 and 129 Fulwell Road were demolished as were Nos 2 and 2A Primrose Cottages. Numerous houses in Primrose Crescent, Roxburgh Street, Laburnum Road, Ronald Square, Enid Avenue, Moray Street and Vivian Square and as far as Side Cliff Road.

The site of Fenwick's Brewery, Low Street, East End.

Fulwell Road was blocked for a while and a suspected unexploded bomb at the crossing was identified as a loaded flare case. The parachute from the mine and four incendiary bombs were recovered.

Two HE bombs fell in Barrack Street in the East End. Five houses were totally wrecked, as was the Scotch Thistle and American Hotel public houses and a Police Box.

Special Constables George Pinkney and Henry Wardle, had already been involved in other rescues near to Fenwick's Brewery when they were called to Barrack Street. Hearing cries for help the pair rescued a woman from buildings on the east side of Barrack Street. The policemen then went to the Scotch Thistle, where they cleared debris from the top of a Morrison shelter, then after partially dismantling the shelter brought out John Howard (67) and his wife Elizabeth (52), but both had been killed and their son John (14), who was seriously injured.

PC John Beadnall (35), was rescued from the wrecked Police Box by wardens Curtis and Farrell.

John Metcalf (34), Doreen and Ethel were rescued from the American Hotel by warden Curtis, while Robert Ross was brought out by warden Cotterill and members of the Rescue Squad.

At No 2 Barrack Cottages, George Thompson (30), his wife Doreen (27), and children George (5) and Doris (3), were killed, while next door at No 3, Elizabeth Scott managed to struggle free from the wreckage of her home.

At No 4, Alice Crawford (44), and her daughters Ruth (15) and Joan (14) were trapped. On duty nearby was warden George Bailey, who without any hesitation began to tunnel into the wreckage. After an hour's hard work, and now assisted by fire guard James Mitcheson, Bailey had succeeded in releasing Mrs Crawford and one of her daughters. Working in a space no more than a foot high, the pair set about rescuing the other girl. Once the girl had been freed from the debris, Bailey, who by now was exhausted, had to be pulled from the tunnel by his feet, dragging the girl behind him.

Bailey, a warden for only 4 months and a joiner by trade at Sunderland Cabinet Works, together with Mitcheson, who worked at Wm Pickersgill & Sons, both had their names published in the *London Gazette* for Gallant Service. ARP controller McIntire stated that: 'The action of fire guard Mitcheson and warden Bailey was more commendable in view of the fact that a large fire had been caused at Greenwell's, near to the incident, which offered a good target for further bombing by the enemy.'

Back on the north side of the river, a 500kg bomb fell in Parkside Terrace, Roker, demolishing Nos 1 to 6. A fire burned under the wreckage at Nos 4 and 5 and at least 6 people were missing.

It wasn't until 8.15 am that Nellie Coxon (49), of No 4, was reported rescued, seriously injured. At 10.20 am, the following day, the body of Isabella Coxon (86), was recovered and at 8.15 am Tuesday the 18th, George Haswell (36), his wife Gladys (37), and sons David (6) and Norman, who was just 12 days old, were reported recovered from the ruins of No 1.

At Gladstone Street, a bomb, estimated as a 250kg, demolished Nos 32, 34, and 36. Casualties were many.

At No 32, Evelyn Briggs (25), Thomas (3), and 6-month-old Michael were killed, and a Miss Briggs and 8-year-old John Briggs were badly hurt.

Lilian Sinclair was killed at No 34, while at No 36 Florence Evans and her daughter June (3), and Sam Johnson (72), lost their lives. Daniel (74) and Emma Warne (64) were also killed in Gladstone Street.

Another parachute mine exploded at the junction of Cairns Road and Newcastle Road, bringing with it the usual devastation.

In his Anderson shelter at his home at 38 Cairns Road, was PC Walter Crosbie, his wife and child, when they were shaken by an explosion close by. Looking around, Crosbie found that his house and many others were badly blast damaged and that a crater in the road, was steadily filling with water due to a burst main. Two houses, Nos 71 and 73, near to the edge of

The shell of the Bright Street Methodist Chapel, Roker.

the crater were completely demolished.

Again, considering the destructive power of the mine, casualties were relatively light. However, Mary Jane Evans (62) was killed at No 71, her husband Edward injured. Next door three people were seriously injured. A number of other people were hurt and about 220 nearby houses were damaged.

Another 500kg bomb hit the edge of the roof at No 6 Netherburn Road, continued through a bedroom window, killing Walter Phillips (37), who was in the room, carried on through the house to the ground floor without exploding. Roads in the immediate area were sealed off, and people evacuated while the bomb was defused.

Incendiaries set fire to the Central Laundry, Roker, causing extensive damage, and another shower of incendiaries completely burned out the Bright Street Methodist Church.

At J.L. Thompson's North Sands shipyard, a 500kg bomb hit the office block and wrecked the old board room and the shipyard stores. Production of the Liberty Ships was not seriously affected. A fire-watcher was blown up a flight of stairs into the shipyard mould loft by blast. Another bomb fell into the river near to Manor Quay and a Firepot fell on the beach next to Thompson's Southwick yard.

Two 1000kg HE, initially thought to be mines, fell in Thompson Park, causing damage to property in surrounding streets.

A 250kg bomb fell at the junction of Givens Street and Cooper Street, Roker, and a 500kg fell on the railway near to the power house situated at the rear of 31 and 33 Givens Street.

Number 41 Southwick Road took a direct hit from a 50kg bomb demolishing the house and damaging those on either side. At Hood Street, witnesses stated that there had been no flash and little sound of an explosion and as there were few traces of an explosion it was first believed that the bomb had not exploded. It was later confirmed as a 50kg bomb and that it had detonated, badly damaging Nos 81 and 83. The occupants were uninjured, being in their shelters.

Probably amongst the most fortunate this night were the residents of Grange

Park Avenue, as at around 2.10 am a parachute mine floated down and came to rest in the front garden of No 9, and didn't explode.

A 250kg HE exploded 80 yards south of North Hylton Road, near to the Borough Boundary, another on the railway at the east end of Westburn Terrace, yet another on the glass works in Portobello Lane, Monkwearmouth, and a 50 kg HE in the railway goods yard opposite. Two bombs fell close together in Fulwell Road and Stansfield Street and a 250kg HE 70 yards south of the North Pier. There was a direct hit on the shelter in Black Road, close to Wearmouth Colliery.

And so, on to the south side of the river. In Perth Road, Plains Farm, a mine exploded at the rear of No 145, killing Mrs Mary Martin (71), who lived at 149, and Annie Bates of No 115. Eighty-one houses in Perth Road alone were damaged, a further 153 in neighbouring streets.

Three HE bombs fell at Ennerdale, Azalea Terrace South and Azalea Avenue, claiming the lives of Lucy (55), and Jean Suffield (15), at 10 Azalea Terrace South. Leonard Salter (80) and Elsie Salter (55), were killed by the bomb in Azalea Avenue.

Nellie Jenson (37), of 103 High Street East managed to get herself out of her blitzed home, even though she was badly injured.

A 50kg bomb demolished 2 Allonby Street, killing Luke Winter (57) and seriously injured his wife Ellen. At this incident it was first thought that an unexploded bomb of a much larger calibre had done the damage, but scorch marks from the explosion were later found.

Fenwick's Brewery in Low Row, was hit and demolished, 2 fire-guards being lucky to escape.

Firepots and incendiaries raided down on Sunderland. The King's Theatre in Crowtree Road was completely burned out as was the Avenue Paint Works in Sawburn Street. Others fell near to the Eye Infirmary in Queen Alexandra Road.

Casualties may have been doubled had it not been for the 32 uxb's, including half of the 10 parachute mines that fell. These were at Waldron Square, off Ryhope Road, No 9 Grange Park Avenue, two in fields at Tunstall Hill Farm and in Silksworth Lane near to the Borough Boundary. It wasn't until the following week that they had all been made safe. The all-clear sounded at 3.12 am.

Just 8 days later, on Monday, 24th May, the carnage and destruction was repeated.

At 2.37 am 'purple' warning was received, followed by the sirens sounding at 2.49 am. The all-clear was at 4.07 am.

During a 40 minute period, beginning at 2.55 am, 10 parachute mines, 56 high-explosive, seven Firepots, two phosphorus and approximately 600 incendiaries were dropped on the town.

Pobably the first incident was at 2.55 am when a 50kg HE bomb fell in the front garden of No 4 Villette Path, Hendon, the resulting explosion practically demolishing Nos 3 and 4 and badly damaging No 5. A further 100

A small statue, now in the grounds of Southmoor School, which thanks God for the failure of a parachute mine to detonate.

houses were damaged, but there were no casualties.

Around 3.05 am, a 500kg bomb fell in Mainsforth Terrace, 50 yards east of St Barnaba's Church, Suffolk Street, demolishing a bakery and a shop, several houses and; setting fire to a fractured gas main.

Ten minutes later, two bombs fell close together, both 500kg, in Hedley Street and Ravensworth Terrace.

In Hedley Street, the bomb fell at No 24 and caused the death of the youngest person killed during the bombing of Sunderland, eleven-day-old Christina Price, who lived at No 35. Christina had been in a Morrison shelter with her father, a soldier home on leave, her mother and two other women. Also at No 24, nineteen-year-old Ethel Tate was killed.

At No 23, Mr Briggs was found in the middle of the wreckage shouting: 'My missus is in there somewhere,' but his 'missus' Mary (58), had been killed.

The bomb which fell in Ravensworth Street claimed the lives of Sarah Ann (or Annie) Watson (42), and Thomas Watson (19), of No 41. Many incendiary bombs had fallen in this area and the Watson brothers, Thomas and Edward were fire watchers and had been fighting fires, when Edward was blown off a roof by blast from a HE and was injured. Thomas was trapped in the same wreckage, but was soon released and followed his brother to hospital, but later died. Soon afterwards the boys' mother was killed by a direct hit on their own house. Mr Watson, on duty as an air raid warden, told the *Sunderland Echo* the following day: 'I visited one or two spots where incidents had occurred before I came to our street and found that my own house had gone. I had been helping put fires out and knew that my sons had been injured, but it was a little time before I knew I had lost my wife.'

John Atkinson of No 42, died from his injuries the following day.

At 3.14 am, another 500kg HE demolished Nos 6, 7, 8 and 9 Robinson Street, Hendon. People were trapped in the debris. At No 6 the Leng and the Bergson families were trapped in a shelter which had collapsed. It is hard to imagine the scene of horror that greeted rescue workers as they removed debris to find two families all but wiped out. Eleven people, seven of them under the age of 13 were killed. Sarah (Belle) Leng was the only survivor, though seriously injured. William Leng (32), Kenneth (8), James (8), 3-year-olds Ruth and William and 15-month-old Marjorie all died together with David Bergson (48), his wife Miriam (46), Arnold (6) and Lillian and Millie Michaelson (13).

At No 7 the Kish family were more fortunate though being seriously injured and next door at No 8 Thomas Jackson (67), was killed.

In Herrington Street, at No 116, more youngsters were victims. Lillian (16) and Olive Swales were killed, their sister Dorothy (13) was seriously injured.

Around 3.10 am a large calibre HE bomb or possibly a parachute mine fell at No 71 Queen Alexandra Road, demolishing Nos 71, 73 and 75.

In their shelter at No 71 were Thomas (50) and Sarah (56) Thompson, both fire-watchers and standing by for the call to duty, and their daughters Hannah Margaret (24) and Eunice (17). Their shelter was wrecked by the explosion and all were trapped.

At No 73 were Rudolph (45), and Margaret Ryan (40), and at No 75 lived Dr Ethel Browell (39), and her mother Mary (70). All were in their shelters. Dr Browell was then in charge of the First Aid Post attached to the Municipal Hospital, and her normal occupation was Senior Assistant Medical Officer of Maternity and Child Welfare in Sunderland. Dr Browell's shelter was on the edge of the crater.

Arriving at the scene within two minutes of the explosion and while bombs were still falling, rescuers found Dr Browell already assisting Mr Thompson,

In October 1941 and in February 1942, Sunderland held Tank Week, where various tanks and armoured vehicles were put on display at the Garrison Field, behind the police station.

Women shipyard workers on board a ship on the River Wear.

Warship Week in Sunderland.

who was killed. They then tried to extricate Hannah, but found they needed more help, but these rescue attempts were in vain, as when Hannah was recovered 'she was past human aid.'

Dr Browell then helped to place a blanket under Mrs Thompson and once rubble was removed she was lifted out, Dr Browell then attended her injuries.

The doctor then returned to her mother, who was also injured and then reported to her first aid post where she treated many others before collapsing from shock.

Many witnesses to her actions, including air raid wardens were compelled to report to the authorities of Dr Browell's work and she was subsequently highly commended in the *London Gazette* for gallant service.

In Corporation Road, Hendon, a 50kg HE demolished Nos 37 and 39 but there were no casualties. Initailly the police officer who examined the debris surmised that the bomb had not exploded, as windows within 10 yards of impact were intact, little shrapnel damage and localised wreckage. The suspected uxb was confirmed by a BDO at 5.10am, however, the bomb is listed as having detonated.

Between 3.10 am and 3.20 am two HE bombs, estimated at 250kg, fell on waste ground, on the south side of the river, a few yards west of Queen Alexandra Bridge. The first struck the cement footpath on the east side of the loop road which joins the New Pallion Road, approximately 30 yards from the clockhouse end of the bridge.

At 4.40 am it was reported by wardens to PC Abbs, that a human leg had been found near the entrance of the Doxford shelter about 40 yards from the crater. Nearby was the body of war reserve Thomas Edward Eves (42). Mr Eves, a former County hockey player had been seen standing close to the clockhouse entrance at the south end of the bridge moments before the bombs exploded. Shrapnel marks can still be seem on a wall at the Pallion end of the bridge. The second bomb fell 80 yards away near the railway in Ogden's Lane on the south side of New Pallion Road.

On the north side of the river, two 500kg HE fell in the Bonnersfield area, one of which fell on or near to the Bromarsh Cinema, trapping many people in the shelter there, bursting a water main. Three people were killed and 19 injured.

A number of houses were demolished or badly damaged and people were trapped in the wreckage. George Brown of 1 Bonnersfield was killed at Bromarsh shelter and of No 2 Millie Humble (19), Marjorie (8), Frederick (7), Doris (4) and 2-year-old Jean were all killed at Bonnersfield shelter, their mother Elizabeth (39), and sisters Mary (11) and Lilian (4) were seriously injured. Joseph Jobling (40) of No 70 and Ellen Morgans (19) also lost their lives. William Middlemiss (42) of No 3 died from his injuries on 25th May.

Two more 500kg HE fell on Abbs Street and Devonshire Street at around 3.10 am.

In Abbs Street the bomb dropped fell at Nos 13 to 16, killing fire-watchers John (45) and Anne (40) Sillett of No 14 and fire-guard Ernest Goldsworthy (46), at No 15, demolishing 8 houses.

In Devonshire Street, the bomb fell at, or close to Nos 1 to 7, killing fire-guard John Simpson (23) and Mary Hughes (73), both at No 4. Virtually every house in the street suffered damage, 12 being totally demolished. A total of 19 people were injured at these incidents.

Shortly before 3.15 am, a parachute mine fell at the junction of Salem Avenue and Harrogate Street, Hendon, setting fire to a fractured gas main. Thirteen houses were demolished and there were fatalities at No 5 Salem Avenue where 70-year-old Dorothy Bickford lost her life, Charles (74) and

Margaret (73) Thompson and Winifred Tuddenham (47), who died the following day, at No 6. The last person to be recovered at 3.10 pm the 25th was 18-year-old Maurice Gallerstein of No 8. Parts of the mine were recovered and taken to the warden's post in Mowbray Road.

Five minutes later another mine fell in Gorse Road off Stockton Road, demolishing houses in Carlyon Street, The Elms North and Ashmore Terrace. Fire-guard Bewicke Ward of 8 Ashmore Terrace was killed and 7 others were injured.

Two 250kg HE fell in Bishopwearmouth Cemetery, damaging the Lodge Cottages and other buildings, killing a horse stabled there.

Two parachute mines drifted to earth at J.L. Thompson's Shipyard at Manor Quay. One caused damage to works buildings, shattering a number of sheds and much of the gatehouse. A fire broke out which was tackled by the fireboat *Fire King* and was brought under control in an hour. The second mine fell between 2 ships lying at the fitting-out quay. The inside vessel, *Silver Park* was badly damaged and the other ship, a Liberty ship named *Denewood* broke from her moorings and had settled on the river bed, fortunately not in a position as to block the river, the water not being deep enough to cover her decks. Both the *Fire King* and *Fire Queen* vessels and the river station next to Thompson's Yard were damaged by bullets and cannon fire.

A stick of four 50kg HE fell close together, in Chester Road, opposite No 14 Westlands, No 1 Priory Grove, in Barnard Street and to the rear of Barnard Street and Abingdon Street. All these bombs were reported initially as 500kg and unexploded, but the War Department was informed that all had exploded, by 4.56 am. Damage to housing near to impact points was considerable.

The Lodge Terrace, shelter, Hendon, where fifteen people were killed.

In the Hendon area a 500kg HE came to earth at the junction of Wear Street and Moor Street around 3.10 am, demolishing 11 houses and trapping 4 people in a shelter. One person, Thomas Taylor (63) was billeted at 63 Wear Street and seven others injured.

One of the better-known bombing incidents took place at 3.15 am in Lodge Terrace, Hendon. All but 3 of the dwellings in Lodge Terrace were single storied houses, having small back yards with no room to build individual shelters. As the night raids started the residents received permission to use the underground shelter at the nearby Glaholm & Robson Rope Works, as the nearest public shelter was situated on the town moor. Many of the residents thought this was too far to go, especially carrying infants and babies an so petitioned to have a surface shelter built in the street. The only possible location for this was at the east end of the street, next to the railway line that ran from the docks to the main lines, next to a rail bridge and close to a rail marshalling area and of course the docks, all legitimate targets.

The shelter was built of double and in some places treble thicknesses of bricks, with a reinforced concrete roof and floor, the roof being 8-10 feet thick. A blast wall ran along the south side where the access door was located. Doors were covered by thick blankets to keep light in and cold out. Divided into compartments, some residents selected the same one on every visit.

The bomb, a 250kg, landed just outside the blast wall, at the south west corner, destroying the wall and first 2 compartments and damaging the others, cantering the shelter over by about 15 degrees. The aircraft that dropped the bomb was heard to dive, the roar of its engines being clearly heard as it pulled out of the dive. The bomb did not scream, but fell with a swooshing sound of rushing air and exploded with a dull thud. Around 40 people were in the shelter. Many of those on fire-watching duty nearby were totally unaware that the shelter had been hit until they were alerted by youngsters Billy Hutchinson and Bill Miller who had managed to get out of the shelter. Nearby was fire-watcher William Ord who described: 'It was an awful scene. The shelter had been ripped right open and huge blocks of concrete were lying about in confusion. We could hear the injured people moaning among the wreckage.'

Many of the residents of Lodge Terrace who had been fire watching had family members in the shelter and using the light from a nearby fire, they clawed at the concrete with their bare hands until heavier equipment arrived. Arthur Sweeting, a holder of the Distinguished Conduct Medal from the Great War, on duty with the Home Guard, helped to dig his wife May from the rubble. May suffered severe blast injuries to her face and spent two months in hospital. She recalled being: 'raised off the ground and buried.' She was trapped for about an hour, and lay all that time next to a boy who had been killed.

Bill Harris remembered: 'We had just got into the shelter. There was no explosion as such. The shelter just disintegrated. I remember being stuck under a wall with my mother and my sisters.'

John Lorenson propped up part of the roof with his back until rescuers arrived. Most of the cottages had their windows blown out and ceilings down and 2 houses were completely destroyed.

Killed were: Eva Thorne (15) of No 4, Frank (60) and Agnes (57) O'Neil of No 6, Ronald McArdle (11) of No 7, Robert Scott (60) of No 8, David Lorenson (65) of No 9, George (50) and Margaret Foster (40) of No 13, Annie Gisby (63) of No 14, brothers Allan and Ronnie Hutchinson aged 15 and 14, of No 15, Susan Hall (43) of No 17, Catherine Telfer (12) of No 20, Anne Huntley (6) and Ann Miller (58) of No 25 and Hannah Warde (67) of 17 Clarke Street.

Another equally horrific incident took place about five minutes after the bomb at Lodge Terrace. Initially listed as a parachute mine, but this was later amended to a 1000kg. Whatever it was, it fell on the east side of St George's Square, the resulting explosion claimed, 18 lives. Six houses were completely devastated, Nos 6 to 11, a further 50 badly damaged and other buildings including West Park Central School, the Masonic Temple, Grange House and Park Road Methodist Church all suffered damage. The Incident Post was set up at 18 St George's Square and later moved to 15 Box and wasn't closed until 9.10 pm Wednesday, 2nd June. It took

At least fifteen more people were killed at St George's Square, off Stockton Road.

Firemen damping down fires at St George's Square.

rescue squads, some from as far away as Birtley, Crook and Willington, many days to recover those killed, and in fact 2 people were never recovered. An inquest held on 2nd July for Anna Rae (61) and Dr. Elizabeth Sharpe-Smith (38) concluded: 'Presumed killed by enemy action.'

Serious fires raged in among the ruins of 2 of the houses, which took almost 8 hours to extinguish and this and live electric cables greatly hampered rescue efforts.

In a letter to the coronor from the Borough Engineer J.E. Lewis to the Controller, dated June 8th, states: 'During the period May 24th to 28th portions of bodies were found on the above incident. On 29th and 30th May 11 badly mutilated bodies were recovered, and from the May 30th to date the site has been cleared. All debris has been turned over, and thorough search made of the basements. No further bodies or portions of bodies have been found. The site is being cleared and levelled and there does not appear to be possible hope of finding any parts of the bodies of persons still believed to be missing.'

The largest crater in Sunderland was in Dun Cow Street, next to the Empire Theatre.

The people who were killed were at No 6 Mrs Ethel Brown (65) and Elizabeth Fallon (45) who died of her injuries on the 25th May. Next door at No 7 Mrs Sarah Garrick (75) and her daughter Miss Leonora Garrick (52). John Pigg (42) his wife Eve, Mrs Margaret Pigg (31) and children Norman (6), and Joyce (11) plus Mrs Margaret Coffey (68) and Ellen Crosby-Simmons (66) all lost their lives at No 8.

The 2 women of which no trace was found, lived at No 9, while Mrs Winifred Cowe (28), at No 11 and at No 12 9-month-old Norma Thompson,

Church Walk, next to Bishopwearmouth Church.

Thomas Gaffney (70), were killed. Mrs Annie Hunter (38) and son Frederick (12) and Mrs Elizabeth Ann Forster (49) also lost their lives.

The biggest crater made in Sunderland resulted from a 1000kg HE falling at Moats Houses, Dun Cow Street, close to the Empire Theatre, measuring 99 feet across by 40 feet deep. The explosion shattered a static water tank and hurled pieces into the air, one section going over the Police Station and into the Garrison Field. No-one was hurt, but damage was caused to Bishopwearmouth Church and the Alms Houses on The Green. The elderly who lived there, were too infirm to make use of shelters.

A 500kg HE fell in Hylton Street West, destroying 4 large shops and badly damaging many more.

Another large HE fell into the ruins of the Binns store, destroyed in the bombing in April 1941, making a large crater over the road from the east side, tearing up tram lines and bringing down overhead cables.

A similar sized bomb to the one that fell in St George's Square fell in Stratford Avenue, Grangetown, demolishing six houses, but no-one was hurt.

Half a dozen HEs fell on the beach and lower promenade at Roker, one of which was causing some consternation some 20 years later, when witnesses sought confirmation that a bomb did not lie dormant in Roker.

During the raid, fire-guard officer Peter Harle was on duty in St George's Terrace, close to the junction with South Cliff. On some steps opposite were leading fireman Charles McManus, a Dr Court and warden and light-house keeper William Emmerson. Part-time warden John George Emms responsible for No 2 Group on the north side of the river, was on duty at the warden's post situated at St Aidan's Church.

All these men could hear the drone of enemy aircraft overhead, and Harle stated: 'I heard the whistling sound of bombs falling', while McManus and Dr Court heard a 'swishing sound of a bomb.' All the men took what cover they could.

Harle went on: 'I heard 2 explosions and a dull thud. I then got up and went to examine the damage to the top of the footpath leading down the grass bank to the lower promenade.'

Harle and the others found that the drinking fountain situated on the bank top, facing Roker Terrace, had been uprooted and deposited on the lower prom. Where the fountain had stood was a crater. The water pipe to the fountain was then pumping out quantities of water. The concrete balustrade had been damaged, but there was little debris where the fountain had been and Harle said: "There was no smell of there having been an explosion."

The incident was roped off and some residents living nearby may have been evacuated, but if they were, all were quickly allowed back into their homes.

The following day Corporation workmen filled in the crater and despite talking to an army BDO, Harle was left with the thought of a uxb in the grass bank on the sea front at Roker.

Head warden Emms, on making enquiries to Thornholme was told that a BDO had examined the site and was now reported safe.

All except Harle accepted the BDO's opinion that a bomb, possibly of small calibre, had hit the fountain and balustrade, bounced off and exploded either in mid-air or on the beach.

Twenty years later, almost to the day, Peter Harle tried to have the site reinvestigated, but due to statements of other witnesses it was decided that the bomb had in fact exploded.

Bombs that fell close to this incident included a 500kg HE, 2 HEs, type unknown and one 50kg exploded on the beach, a 250kg exploded on the lower promenade (possibly the one Harle thought an uxb) and an ABB 500 incendiary container found on the beach.

A mine fell into the river near to No 14 Staiths. A 500kg HE exploded at the North Eastern Marine in South Docks and together with a 250kg caused a 25 per cent reduction of production. Another bomb fell into the sea near to the works. Two 250kg HE fell at Hendon Dock, one inside the Monsanto Chemical Works, the other just outside. Some 50kg HE bombs fell at the west end of Hendon Dock Bridge, on No 31 Coal Staith at Hendon Dock and on Hetton Sidings railway at Ayre's Quay. Two bombs fell into Hendon Dock itself and a Firepot fell at the oil storage tanks south of the North Tidal Basin. A ship lying at anchor took a direct hit from a Firepot and in Hudson Dock another ship was hit by a 1,000kg bomb. A smaller boat was holed and sank.

A 50kg HE fell on Hendon gas works, another on the railway at the north-east corner of the gas works and another 150 yards away to the north-east.

Another fell at Wearmouth Colliery Drops near to No 1 Post at the pit. Perhaps more depressing to some were the bombs that fell on local breweries. One fell on Cameron's Brewery in Dunning Street, Fenwick's Brewery in Coronation Street was the recipient of two Firepots and Vaux Brewery was damaged by a 50kg HE.

Ninety-two HE bombs were reported to have been dropped.

This was the last time bombs fell on Sunderland, even though there were two years of war to go. The sirens would sound a few more times and within days of the last two heaviest raids a detachment of barrage balloons arrived, hardly to be used. Large areas of the town had been flattened which made way for post-war development.

Gas Office corner, looking towards the Railway Station.

ON TO VICTORY

A summer fair during 1941 or 42.

Wartime Security

Wartime security in the Northern Region involved both civilian and military authorities including MI5, with all groups meeting regularly to discuss people and incidents that may have had a detrimental effect on the war effort or the morale of the public.

Many incidents were reported in the Sunderland area, including, on 1st December 1940, a 17-year-old youth who was arrested as a result of papers being found on a ship at Doxford's shipyard. These papers suggested that the ship was to be a target for sabotage, followed by German sentences and crude maps of the River Wear showing the position of the ship. The youth was fined £20 for recording information that might be useful to the enemy. This youth also admitted being responsible for the poster found on a builder's hut, on the 15th October claiming that, 'Britain is doomed. Heil Hitler.' The youth's actions were attributed to: 'an unbalanced sense of humour and a desire for notoriety.'

During the same month, a meeting of the *Daily Worker* was noted to have been attended by 50-60 people, where there was criticism of the Government and air raid shelters. A man in RAF uniform was reported to RAF Newcastle.

Another man from Elvington Street, was fined £10, for taking photographs of friends on the sea front at Roker. An innocent pastime you may think, but during the war the sea front had numerous defence structures and guns situated as an anti-invasion measure, and when this film was developed the photographs showed part of these defences.

During March, 1941, Special Branch made inquiries into the origin of a batch of German Newspapers and letters that had been used in packing cases of children's toys received by Binns Store. Some of the papers were dated 1940.

The Security Bulletin for 15th May 1941, stated that efforts were being made to trace a man who telephoned the Regal Cinema, in Holmeside, who, after confirming that a film titled 'Escape' was being shown, then said: 'Then you'll be blasted to hell.'

Even religious groups did not escape being watched. In April, 1941, the Reverend Gibson Salisbury, the Vicar of Eppleton, had his house searched, which turned up information concerning contacts made on holidays. According to the Northern Region Special Branch, Rev Salisbury was known to have pro-German views and had been circulating a weekly letter to troops giving information that may be useful to the enemy.

During October 1941, it was noted that there had been an increase in the activities of Jehovah's Witnesses in Sunderland, and that they were making headway in the town and while they could not be described as subversive, concern was felt that each new recruit could become a pacifist.

At the end of June 1943, a man was fined 8 shillings, for not handing in an unexploded incendiary bomb to the police and 2 Sunderland women were severely cautioned for including information of air raid damage in letters stopped by the postal censor.

Security activities were not confined to British subjects. A neutral Swedish sailor, on board the SS *Thyra* berthed in Sunderland, was searched after his ship mates claimed that he expressed anti-British and pro-German views. The search founds two rolls of film, which when processed showed views of ships in convoy at sea and of a ship's deck.

Home Guard using Thompson machine guns, probably at Whitburn camp. The Thompson was a weapon favoured by gangsters during the American prohibition era.

Home Guard bayonet practice, 1941.

Invasion Exercise

'German walked Wearside Streets' ran the headline in the *Sunderland Echo* of Monday 19th October 1942.

This occurred during a large invasion exercise held in Sunderland and surrounding districts which involved regular Army and RAF units as well as Home Guard and Civil Defence.

The 'German' was a soldier dressed in full German uniform who walked the streets of Sunderland for over an hour and a half before being apprehended.

Camouflaged Home Guard machine gun position, 1942.

The objectives of the exercise was to test the defences of the town against not only air raids, but from assault by invading land forces.

The defenders, mainly Home Guard units, had to act against heavy air raids, simulated by RAF planes flying low over the town, which had knocked out one of the bridges over the Wear, hampering transport. Acts of sabotage had to be dealt with. These included a WREN with fake identification cards gaining access to a Civil Defence Control Centre and causing damage and a soldier supposedly out jogging being caught spying. Members of the Civil Defence had to cope with around 30 air raid incidents with others being reported in Washington, Boldon, Whitburn and Castletown.

It was assumed that the attackers – regular army – had gained a foothold to the west and were keen to capture a port to allow reinforcements by sea. Other

Invasion Exercises held in the South Durham Street area, Hendon, on Sunday 16th October.

House to house fighting. Note children that hampered the exercises.

attacks came from the north and south and made ground but at heavy cost. Artillery pieces were brought up to a vantage point overlooking the town, but a Home Guard unit hiding nearby captured them and their crews. Fierce battles were fought for control of 'two hills' on the outskirts of the town and at one village the defenders were so strong at beating off attacks that umpires had to intervene and disqualify them to allow the attackers to reach their objectives before the exercise ended.

Eventually, the attackers forced their way into the town and street fighting broke out, with blank rounds, smoke bombs and thunder-flashes adding to the realism, However, onlookers, especially children, proved to be a hindrance and some were reportedly lucky not to have been injured.

All the objectives were reached, but at such a cost that it was concluded that the attackers would not be able to defend against a determined counter-attack and despite some being on duty for 15 hours, all thought it was a valuable experience.

Refreshments for some of those taking part in the exercise, probably Home Guard.

To the victor the spoils, German U-boat U776, enters the Wear in 1945.

The mayor of Sunderland, Councillor Young, looking through the periscope of the U776, watched by Town Clerk Mr McIntire.

The Mayor of Sunderland, Councillor John Young, announces the end of the war in Europe.

The announcement of the end of hostilities in Europe – VE Day – was heralded by a fanfare of trumpets and a speech by the Mayor, Councillor John Young from the steps of the Town Hall in Fawcett Street on Tuesday, 8th May, 1945. The Police Brass band played before and after the announcment and the National Anthem was sung with great fervour by the crowd which was estimated to be around 10,000 people.

Shops and businesses were covered in bunting and the flags of the victorious countries. Streets were decked out for parties and some houses had flags flying, but it was noted in the *Sunderland Echo* that one house in Hylton Road had black ribbons in the centre of the decorations to mark their own tragedy. But despite the heavy rain at times, street parties were held with ex-POWs and servicemen and women as guests of honour.

Some sailors took the celebrations a bit far by firing off a gun on a ship berthed on the Wear. Around a dozen 20mm anti-aircraft shells fell in the Roker and Fulwell areas damaging houses, but no-one was hurt.

VJ Day or Victory over Japan, on Tuesday, 14th August, saw the Mayor making an another announcement from the Town Hall steps this time at 1 am. After the subdued celebrations of VE Day, thought to have been because of many local servicemen being POWs of the Japanese and some were still fighting, Wearsiders partied for much of the early morning and rest of the day. One person described it as 'First footing in August'. Police had to rescue one youth from a ledge on a building opposite the Town Hall after he became stuck. Now the war was over.

Flags and bunting mark the end of the war in Europe.

VE Day fancy dress.

Policemen having to hold back the crowds in Fawcett Street.

Crowds gather in the rain in Fawcett Street to hear the announcement of the end of hostilities.

Dancing in Mowbray Park on VE Day.

*King George VI and the Mayor, Myers Wayman, inspect Civil Defence personnel
in John Street in June 1943.*

The People's History

To find out more about this unique series of local history books – and to
receive a catalogue of the latest titles – send a large stamped addressed
envelope to:

**The People's History Ltd
Suite 1
Byron House
Seaham Grange Business Park
Seaham
County Durham
SR7 0PY**